Holding the Circle

By Arts Equity Collective

(Community- Centered Support for Suicidal Youth)

Holding the Circle
By Arts Equity Collective

(Community- Centered Support for Suicidal Youth)

***Blanket Toss* by Don Henry**

Title: Holding the Circle: Community- Centered Support for Suicidal Youth

ISBN: 979-8-9991783-2-9
Published by: Arts Equity Collective
Printed in the United States of America

Edited by: Arts Equity Collective
Cover Design: Adam Hayden
Cover Art: *Blanket Toss* by Don Henry

Dedication

This book is dedicated to the Maniilaq Health Association of Kotzebue, Alaska. Your partnership with Arts Equity Collective has strengthened the work of suicide prevention across Alaska Native and American Indian communities carrying some of the heaviest loss and the deepest resilience.

Our time together in the 8-hour, in-person K.C. Suicide Prevention Train-the-Trainer workshop brought Behavioral Health Specialists, Putnak Foster Care Workers, regional educators, and local advocates into one circle of commitment. The insights you shared helped shape this publication into a resource that honors culture, land, and region-specific realities.

Arts Equity Collective exists to ensure that all people are heard, protected, and creatively represented. Through workshops, authorship, and community-rooted practices, we work to uplift marginalized voices and equip both seasoned professionals and newcomers with practical tools to prevent suicide and strengthen families.

Within these pages, you'll find guidance for mental health workers, strategies for supporting parents and caregivers, contributing factors that increase youth suicide ideation, effective approaches to suicide prevention, wellness activities, and arts-based approaches that help young people process pain, speak their truth, and begin healing. To bring Arts Equity Collective's K.C. Suicide Prevention Program to your school, organization, or community, please contact president, MoPoetry Phillips at mopoetry@artsequitycollective.org, or visit www.artsequitycollective.org.

About the Curriculum

Arts Equity Collective's *Holding the Circle: Community-Centered Support for Suicidal Youth* curriculum was created for those working in suicide prevention with youth and teens in grades K–12, as well as anyone seeking to become trauma-informed and prepared to support someone in crisis. It utilizes the K.C. Suicide Prevention Program's evidence-aligned behavioral health strategies combined with culturally responsive, trauma-informed creative tools proven effective in both rural and urban communities, including high-risk regions facing severe social, economic, and historical challenges.

If you are a Behavioral Health Specialist, Peer Recovery Supporter, Mental Health First Aid Responder, educator, foster care worker, or anyone serving children and families, this book is designed for you. It supports your practice, strengthens your resilience, and helps you avoid burnout, compassion fatigue, and the emotional exhaustion that often accompanies crisis work. It provides the endurance and clarity needed to continue showing up for youth with compassion, consistency, and cultural humility.

Inside, you will find accessible checklists that help identify suicide warning signs, risk factors, and indicators of cyberbullying, along with national and community-specific hotline resources. The curriculum includes dedicated prevention tools for American Indian and Alaskan Native communities, and resources intentionally designed to "open more and more doors of communication." You will learn strategies to help families build healthier dialogue and create nonverbal suicide-prevention tools that can interrupt crisis moments and save lives.

This curriculum also introduces arts-based suicide-prevention practices that teach youth how to identify and articulate emotions, self-regulate, and harness creative expression as a path toward safety and healing. Teens are guided through Therapeutic Writing practices using literary devices for reflection and release; Close Reading and thematic exploration using powerful poetry and prose from authors living in Kotzebue, Alaska, alongside diverse voices nationwide; and a range of Mindfulness Activities including breathwork, grounding techniques, and

About the Curriculum (cont.)

Visual Arts Analysis exercises. The book features original artwork, including pieces by Alaskan visual artist, Don Henry, to support visual learning, cultural connection, and emotional engagement.

Holding the Circle is more than a curriculum—it's a commitment. A commitment to hold space for youth when the world feels heavy, to equip adults with tools that honor both culture and compassion, and to ensure that no child walks through their darkest moments alone. Within these pages, you are invited to join a community of caregivers and educators who believe in prevention, healing, and the transformative power of creative expression. This work saves lives—one conversation, one classroom, one circle at a time.

Contents

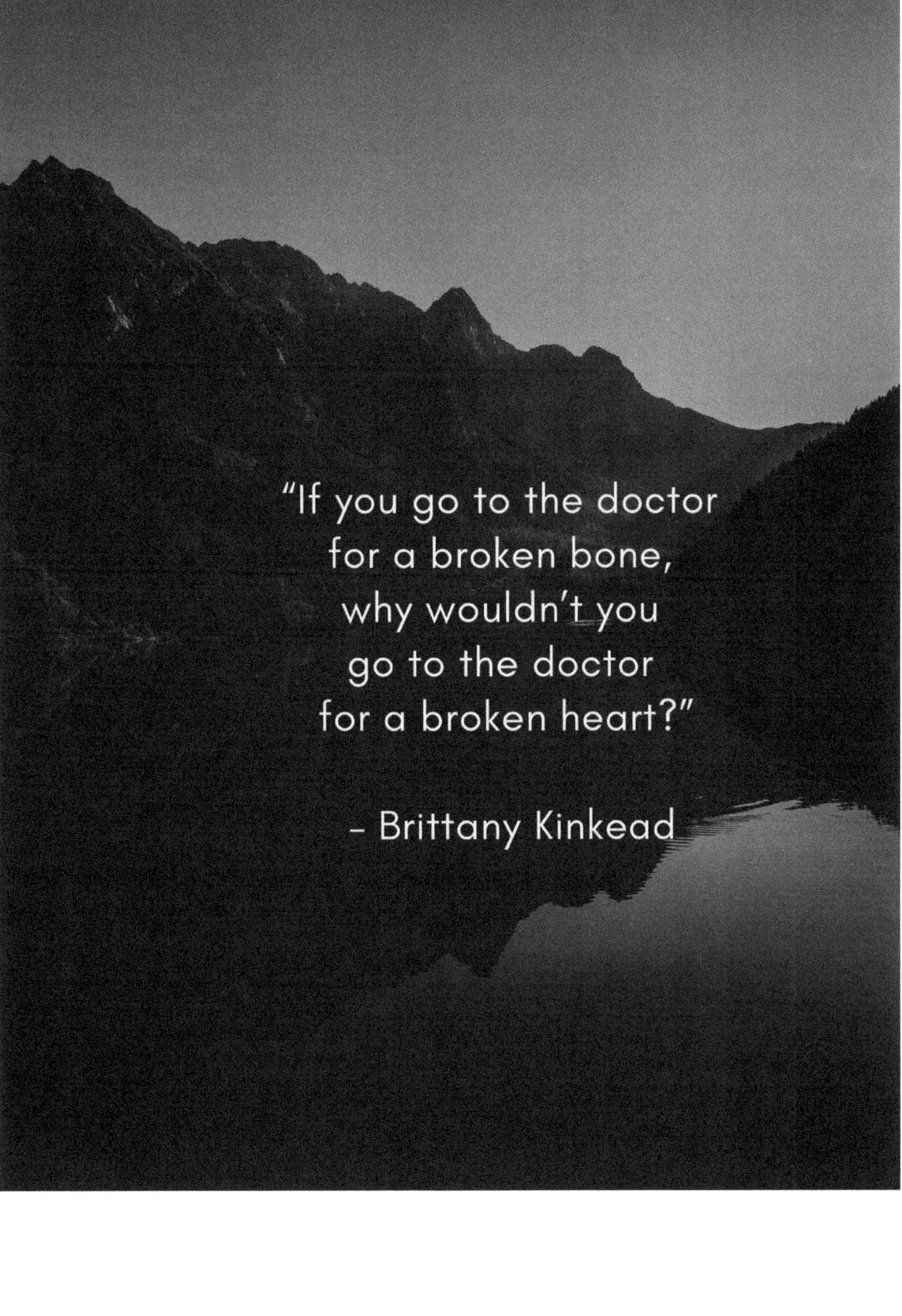
"If you go to the doctor
for a broken bone,
why wouldn't you
go to the doctor
for a broken heart?"

- Brittany Kinkead

Hush Hurts: A Trilogy of Staying
By Ramica Babers- BluPoetry

They told you, "Hush."
And the world went quiet-
but the ache kept whispering.

You tried to speak,
to say that the night felt heavy,
that the words at school stuck like thorns,
that the mirror didn't clap anymore.
They said, "You're fine."
But fine felt like shrinking.

That's how hush hurts.
It teaches the heart to hold its breath.
It makes silence sound holy
when really, it's lonely.

You start believing the lie
that nobody would understand.
You start smiling in public
and fading in private.

But listen-
you don't have to disappear
to make the pain stop.
You don't have to stay silent
to stay loved.

Talk.
Even if it shakes.
Even if it comes out sideways.
Because every word you speak
is a light switch in the dark.

Tell a teacher, a friend, a nurse,
someone whose eyes feel kind.
They can help you find a door
when the walls start closing in.

Your voice is not trouble.
Your truth is not too loud.
You are not broken-
you are blooming.

Hush hurts-
but speaking heals.
And somewhere,
someone is waiting to hear your story,
so they can choose to stay too.

Evening Serenity **by Don Henry**

The Arctic Reality of Youth Suicide

Alaska holds a painful distinction. According to the Center for Disease Control and Prevention, youth ages 10–24 die by suicide here at a rate twice as high as in the rest of the United States. The numbers alone feel stark, but behind them is a landscape that shapes lives in ways people outside the Arctic rarely understand.

For those born in the Far North, extreme daylight and long stretches of darkness become part of the body's vocabulary, something endured, adapted to, folded into daily life. Survival teaches you not to notice the sky too much. But for those of us who have lived in warmer regions, where daylight drifts gently between nine and fifteen hours depending on the season, the Arctic rhythm hits differently.

The contrast is sharp enough to feel in your bones. Your body knows the truth long before your mind does. Darkness triggers the internal clock, whispering that it's time to rest. Melatonin rises. Muscles soften. This is the ancient choreography our biology depends on. When that rhythm is disrupted, when night lingers for weeks or daylight refuses to leave, it doesn't just change sleep. It changes mood, resilience, and emotional balance. Sleep deprivation worsens depression, heightens stress responses, intensifies negative thinking, and leaves young people especially vulnerable to feelings of hopelessness and suicide ideation.

We cannot command the sun to rise earlier. But we can acknowledge the truth: some regions carry environmental burdens that directly affect mental health. These forces do not act alone, but they intertwine with history, culture, trauma, and community in a way that demands a new kind of understanding. If we want to save lives in the Arctic, we need a region-specific path that starts with awareness, honors the realities of place, and moves with both courage and compassion. This book is an invitation to walk that path.

Respect for elders in Alaskan Native and American Indian communities moves far beyond the Western idea of aging. In Alaska, elder voices are not simply valued, they are foundational. Elders hold the stories that anchor identity, the wisdom shaped by generations of survival, and the cultural knowledge that keeps communities rooted even through profound change.

So, the first step in creating this publication was not to look outward, but inward toward the people who have carried these truths the longest. We sat with a circle of elders and asked a single, urgent question, **"What do you believe is driving our youth and teens to attempt or die by suicide?**

Their answers were not abstract theories; they were lived understandings born from decades of watching their communities grow, struggle, and endure. Those conversations formed the backbone of what follows. As we weave in the suicide prevention strategies from Arts Equity Collective's K.C. Suicide Prevention Plan, we will move through the nine categories that emerged from the elders' reflections. Each one of these are a vital strand in understanding both the harm and the hope within Alaska's youth. Turn to the index on page 123 for the complete list of "Reasons Youth and Teens Attempt and/or Die by Suicide."

1. **Poverty, Injustice, & Social-economic Stressors**
2. **Feeling Unheard and Invalidated**
3. **Lack of Coping Skills & Emotional Regulation**
4. **Loneliness, Isolation, & Not Finding Their Tribe**
5. **Trauma Exposure (Personal, Family, or Community)**
6. **Mental Health Stigmas & Cultural Barriers**
7. **Social Media Pressure & Unrealistic Standards**
8. **Hopelessness & Lack of Future Vision**
9. **Lack of Supportive Relationships & Safe Adults**

*Poverty, Injustice, & Social-economic Stressors

- Poverty, homelessness, unavailable or inadequate housing, and job loss
- Injustice and discrimination
- Social-economic struggle, lack of health resources, and lack of educational opportunities
- Overwhelming real-life pressures with limited support from family and community support
- Isolation
- Lack of healthy resources

Alaska's high suicide rates cannot be separated from the broader realities of poverty, injustice, and socio-economic stressors that many families face. There is intergenerational trauma from genocide, colonialism, the Boarding School Era, sexual violence, and forced assimilation that American Indians have endured. In addition, when basic needs such as stable housing, consistent employment, and access to medical care are unmet, it creates a pervasive sense of hopelessness. Limited availability of medications, inadequate mental-health resources, and a shortage of trained professionals, especially those who can support youth with learning disabilities, further deepen this crisis. Families navigating homelessness, discrimination, or chronic financial strain often experience overwhelming daily pressures with very little community or institutional support, leaving individuals more vulnerable to emotional distress and suicidal ideation.

Addressing suicide in Alaska requires acknowledging the intersection of these barriers and approaching prevention through a holistic lens. Bringing together key partners including housing authorities, medical providers, educators, tribal organizations, and mental-health specialists is essential to creating meaningful, systemic change. Suicide prevention cannot be isolated from conversations about access, equity, and resources; instead, it must account for the realities of isolation, lack of healthy coping outlets, and limited opportunities that many Alaskans face. By addressing these foundational needs, communities can strengthen protective factors, restore hope, and create environments where individuals feel supported, seen, and valued.

ILL Legalization: The Sick Times We Are Living In
(Inspired by Paul Scott's Artwork: Posy Vase, No. 2, No Human Being is Illegal)
By: MoPoetry Phillips

You want to protect our borders?
Show me the red, white, and blue,
I'll show the borders
To lands you stole that you migrated to.
It's disingenuous to run others back to their homes.
If everyone except the indigenous had to leave,
We'd ALL be gone-
Back to our foreign homes.

How ironic,
We have squatter's laws
To give others the right to live in places
Where they don't pay mortgage, or rent
Yet, the US proudly used slave labor to build this nation
Along with the labor of immigrants.

Can the US ever be our home?
All the time we've been here,
We've been forced into an unsure position.
Told to go back where we came from-
But only black and brown people are facing eviction.

"No Human Being is Illegal," it reads,
But what could be more illegal?
Perpetuate violence and mistreat law abiding citizens
Round up,
Separate families,
Even a mother and father ... ... from their own child,
Because we refuse to see them as equal.
These are sick times we are living in!
We lack common respect for people.
This is just another slavery sequel.

K.C. Suicide Prevention Warning Signs

SUICIDE WARNING SIGNS

Making Funeral Arrangements

Giving Things Away

Possessing Lethal or Harmful Means

Making Suicide Threats

Searching for Ways to Kill Themselves

Talking/Writing About Wanting to Die

Isolation, Withdrawal, Feeling Alone, or Lost

Increased Use of Alcohols or Drugs

Engaging in Risky Behaviors

Self Harm by Negative Coping Skills like Cutting

Talking About Feeling Trapped or in Unbearable Pain

Drastic Changes in Behavior, Extreme Mood Swings

A Sense of Hopelessness / No Purpose

Talking About Being a Burden

Increased Aggressiveness, Irritability, or Anxiousness

Negative Self View

Arts Equity Collective, P O Box 317746, Cincinnati, OH 45231
Website: www.artsequitycollective.org

K.C. Suicide Prevention Risk Factors

Suicide Risk Factors

- Family history of suicide and/or child abuse
- Previous suicide attempts
- History of mental disorders, especially depression
- History of alchohol or substance abuse disorders
- Cultural and religious beliefs
- Isolation, a feeling of being cut off from other people.
- Barriers to accessing mental health treatment
- Loss (relational, social, work, or financial)
- Easy access to lethal or harmful weapons
- Unwillingness to seek help due to mental health substance/alcohol abuse disorders, or suicide ideation

Arts Equity Collective, P O Box 317746, Cincinnati, OH 45231
Website: www.artsequitycollective.org

Understanding Burnout in Mental Health Professionals

Burnout is a state of prolonged physical, emotional, and mental exhaustion caused by chronic workplace stress, overwhelming demands, or lack of support. For mental health professionals, it often results in reduced effectiveness, emotional depletion, and a diminished capacity to provide compassionate care.

Compassion Fatigue: Key Concepts and Prevention

What Is Compassion Fatigue?

Compassion fatigue is a rapid-onset emotional and physical exhaustion that results from supporting individuals in distress. It develops more quickly than burnout and often appears in professionals who regularly engage in caregiving or crisis response.

Common Symptoms

* Irritability related to the stress or suffering of others
* Feelings of guilt
* Reduced self-care
* Difficulty functioning or concentrating
* Operating on "autopilot"
* Sadness that may be mistaken for depression or trauma

These symptoms emerge when the emotional demands of helping exceed an individual's capacity to recover and reset.

Preventing and Reducing Compassion Fatigue

1. **Maintain Professional Connection-** Regular interaction with colleagues reduces isolation and provides shared understanding. Professional support networks help normalize experiences and promote emotional resilience.

2. **Seek Consultation or Supervision**- Clinical supervision or consultation ensures practitioners receive guidance, accountability, and structured support. It also provides space to process challenging cases and emotions safely.

3. **Use Healthy Venting Practices**- Safe, appropriate venting allows emotional release without causing harm. Practitioners should choose trusted individuals and maintain confidentiality and professionalism.

4. **Practice Gratitude**- Keeping a gratitude journal or log helps shift attention toward positive experiences, improving emotional balance and supporting long-term wellbeing.

Preventing and Reducing Compassion Fatigue (cont.)

5. **Prioritize Self-Care**- Intentional self-care: physical, emotional, spiritual, and creativity is essential. Examples include exercising, resting, engaging in hobbies, and setting healthy boundaries.

6. **Use Personal "Safety Nets"** -Activities or practices that reliably restore emotional stability during overwhelming moments. Identifying these supports before a crisis ensures they are accessible when needed.

These may include:

* Listening to music
* Journaling
* Prayer or meditation
* Reading
* Humor or laughter

7. **Debrief Regularly -** Structured debriefing helps teams process difficult events, maintain communication, and strengthen support systems. Organizations may use meetings or digital tools such as SLACK to facilitate ongoing dialogue and shared reflection.

I. Addressing Suicide Risk Through Lack of Supportive Connections

True Love **by Don Henry**

***Lack of Supportive Relationships & Safe Adults**

- No mentors or trusted adults
- Adults missing signs of distress, turning a blind eye
- Feeling youth or teens are "too young to feel that" or don't know what they are talking about
- Not having anywhere safe to express themselves
- Wanting connection, but not receiving it
- Feeling trapped due to being in a rural area. For example, if teens or youth don't feel supported in rural areas, they are more likely to feel trapped and unsafe.

A child's first bully is an unhealed parent.

Reshared by – Formative Years – Tina Smith-Johnson

www.mastervanikabir.com

Therapeutic Letter Writing by Brittany Kinkead
(Letter to Someone in the Family. Prompt: "I accept"…)

"I accept that I was not able to fall in line with what you had planned for me to suit your personal desires/plans. I accept that my tears were a waste of your emotional time and left you uncomfortable. I accept that your public image and idea of "perfect family' was scarred and forever tainted by the abuse I endured at the hands of many. I accept that your view of tough love was received in my heart, mind, and soul as abuse. I accept that I had to disappoint you in order to find safety and some sense of happiness. I accept that I still love you and forgive you even though that love has been redefined in unbelievable ways. I accept that I have truly failed time and time again. I accept that I'm not perfect and never will be. I accept the need to work on myself daily. I accept the responsibility of breaking "generational traumas and curses." I accept that only I can make my pain mean something deeper than the physical, mental, and emotional scars it has forever left. I accept that I will always love you, but with boundaries and understanding. I lovingly accept the profound responsibility to love my children with genuineness and compassion. I accept the calling to bring love, peace, acceptance, healing, and humor to this heavy and dark world everywhere I go. I accept that my heart, even though it's been shattered and pieced together, should always shine through like a beautiful, textured lamp.

***Feeling Unheard or Invalidated**

- Their voices and feelings aren't heard, especially within their families and communities (This is really true if their viewpoints are different.)
- Adults dismiss or invalidate their feelings.
- Even when adults offer help, youth have a hard time accepting help due to lack of trust
- Not being listened to or taken seriously
- They need us to do more than see them. They want us to hear them.
- They feel invisible
- Youth and teens don't know how to express themselves, so they engage in negative coping skills and risky behaviors.

If Only I Could Explain

By Ari's BAKERY: Beauty About Knowing Every Rare Youth

Life is like a cycle, just wait til dawn.
It goes on and on.
So much beauty in the pain. If only I could explain.
I see beauty hiding behind all the dirt.
Tell me where it hurts.
I see trees bowing and worshiping the true name.
If only I can explain.
Understand that everyone goes through something in life.
You never know what someone is going through.
Unless you've been in their shoes.
Looking for a change just needs to be arranged.
It is like a bird waiting to spread its wings.
If only I could explain.
Life is like a poem, you feel what you feel.
Everything seems so real, but what's the real deal?
Like a song, you can write your story and play along.
If only I can explain, it's like the storm and the rain.
You go through so much pain
Never know what will happen next.
Imagine going before the King of Kings.
Maybe then, you'll see the finer side of things.
Just take a look and see what life really is.

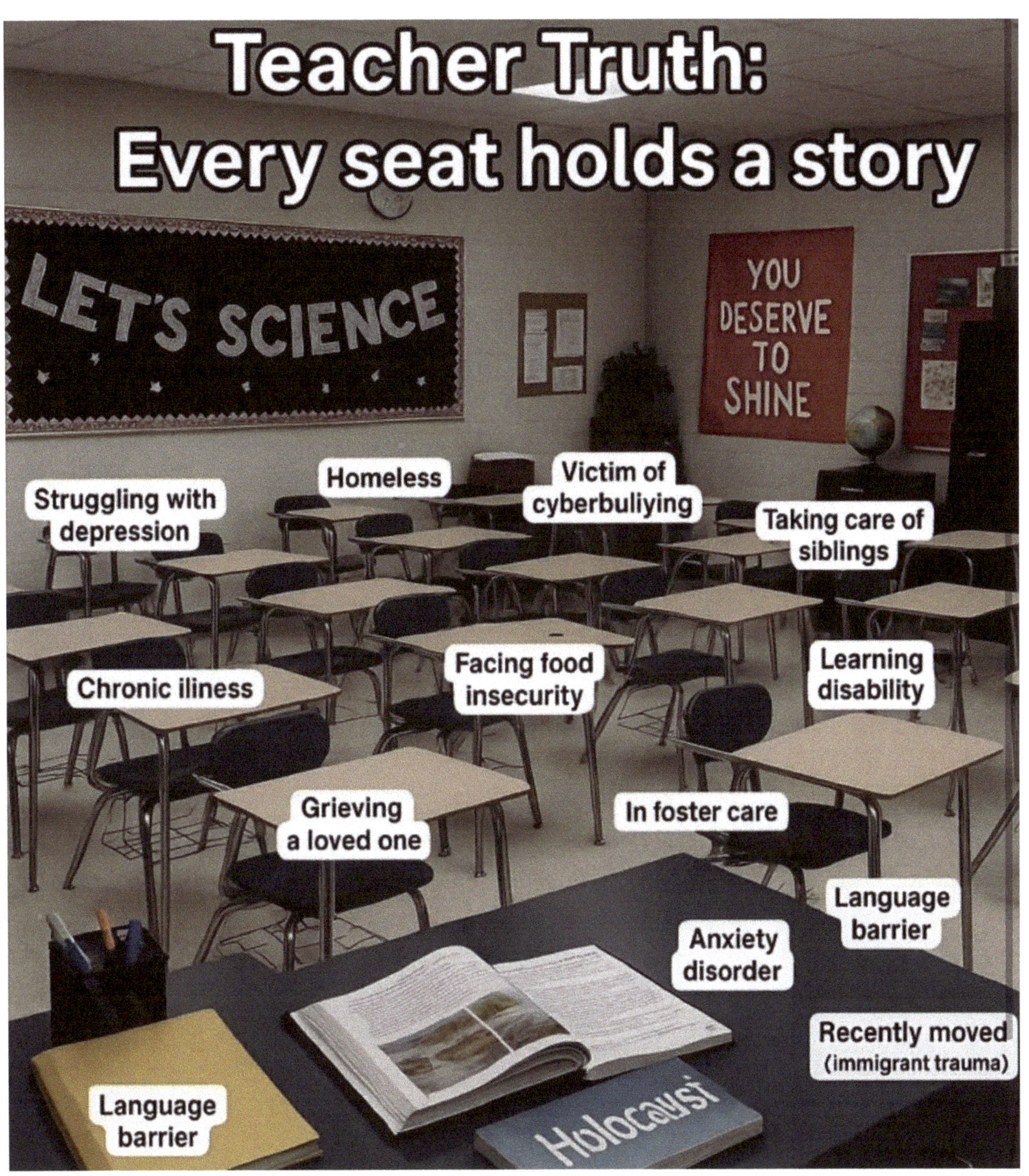
Teacher Truth:
Every seat holds a story
LET'S SCIENCE
YOU DESERVE TO SHINE
Struggling with depression
Homeless
Victim of cyberbuliying
Taking care of siblings
Chronic iliness
Facing food insecurity
Learning disability
Grieving a loved one
In foster care
Language barrier
Anxiety disorder
Recently moved (immigrant trauma)
Language barrier
Holocaust

Therapeutic Letter Writing by Tamara Boyd
(Letter to Myself)

Dear Tamara;

I am grateful to God for creating you with a mind that seeks to serve Him by serving others. I also give thanks to Him for the resilience you have displayed in overcoming challenges both personally and professionally. I thank God for keeping you focused on present opportunities. He has given you the determination to make a difference. I thank God for enabling your mind to have peace that surpasses all understanding which allows you to make decisions by faith and look to Him for a good outcome. Your skills and strength belong to Him. In Him, you live, move, and have your being.

***Lack of Coping Skills & Emotional Regulation**

- Not learning or applying coping techniques
- Not knowing how to handle loss, failure, rejection, and disappointment
- Not knowing how to have self-compassion
- Not knowing how to cope with childhood trauma
- Living in a "crash out" world where everything feels like a crisis (catastrophizing)
- Negative generalizations about life
- Not forming healthy relationships

EMOTION REGULATION STRATEGIES

Name the emotion

Validate the emotion

Identify triggers

Meditation or mindfulness

Talking through emotions

Journalling

SimplyPsychology

Notice when you need a break

Good sleep hygiene

Consider therapy

From Naming to Healing: Teaching Emotional Awareness

As a former Artist in Residence teaching poetry and theatre, I stumbled across a theatre game called "Spaghetti" that quickly became a favorite among youth and teens. Each student received a printed Emotion Chart, or I pulled it up on the Smart Board for everyone to see. I always began by using myself as the example: I'd scan the chart, secretly choose an emotion, and then act it out using only the word spaghetti. If I chose sadness, I'd let my face fall, soften my posture, and whisper "spaghetti" in the most sorrowful tone my body could offer. Their task was to guess the emotion by comparing my performance to the chart.

Then one by one, students selected an emotion, stepped forward, and spoke their single word, "spaghetti", to the room. At first, I thought it was just a lighthearted way to encourage participation. But as I watched them ask about unfamiliar feelings, "What does devastated mean? I realized the game was doing deeper work. It helped them understand, name, and express the emotions living inside them. According to the Emotion Regulation Strategies chart, "naming the emotion" is a key component of emotional regulation. We all experience powerful feelings. Learning how to recognize, express, and respond to them is a skill that isn't automatic, but taught, supported, and practiced.

The hard truth is that we often ask children to regulate emotions we adults once told them to ignore. This pattern can show up in classrooms and discipline practices, shaping how young people are treated when they're overwhelmed or hurt. It's also impossible to ignore the historical context that shapes emotional expression for many communities. Alaskan Native students were taken from their families throughout the 20th century and sent to distant boarding schools.

From Naming to Healing: Teaching Emotional Awareness (cont.)

During this failed, forced assimilation they were punished, often violently, for speaking their languages. Also, their hair was cut, they were stripped of their cultural identity, verbally and physically abused, and in many cases subjected to sexual abuse. The trauma of those years still moves through generations, showing up as grief, depression, substance abuse, and increased vulnerability to suicide ideation. This is why loving, affirming, safe, and culturally respectful learning environments matter to help children unlearn silence, reconnect with their own emotions, and begin healing.

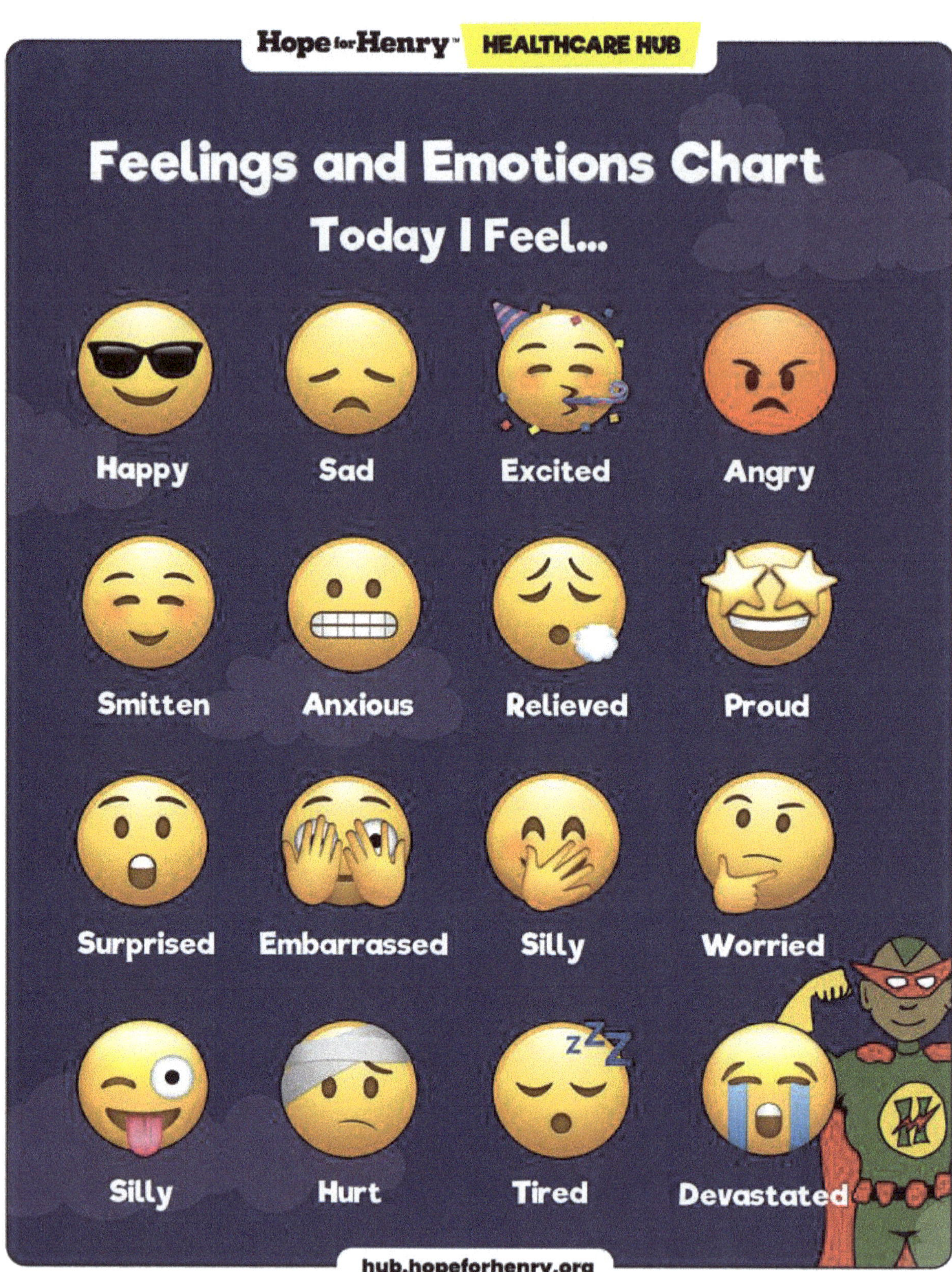
Hope for Henry™ HEALTHCARE HUB
Feelings and Emotions Chart
Today I Feel...
Happy
Sad
Excited
Angry
Smitten
Anxious
Relieved
Proud
Surprised
Embarrassed
Silly
Worried
Silly
Hurt
Tired
Devastated
hub.hopeforhenry.org

GROUNDING TECHNIQUES FOR THE SENSES

5 THINGS YOU CAN SEE

4 THINGS YOU CAN TOUCH

3 THINGS YOU CAN HEAR

2 THINGS YOU CAN SMELL

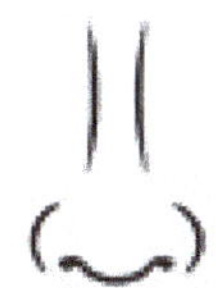

1 THINGS YOU CAN TASTE

Helping Youth Reset and Regain Control

Coping skills are essential tools that help youth practice self-discipline. They teach children to recognize when their emotions are rising and how to pause, breathe, and reset. One of the simplest yet most effective methods is "Grounding Techniques for the Senses."

A third-grade student once came into my classroom with her mother, both visibly shaken. The child was crying so hard she could barely speak, her breath fluttering at the edge of panic. I offered them seats and assured the student that I would help her find the words she couldn't reach.

I began with the 4-7-8 breathing technique: four seconds inhaling through the nose, seven seconds holding, eight seconds releasing. I modeled the rhythm until she eventually joined me. When her breathing finally steadied, I guided her through "Grounding Techniques for the Senses" five things she could see, four she could touch, three she could hear, two she could smell. Taste was harder, so I invited her to imagine herself on a beach and name one thing she would taste. She whispered, "ice cream" and let out a long, relieved breath.

With her body grounded, her voice returned. She told me she was upset about the grade her teacher had given her, that she rarely received praise, and watched other children get candy and encouragement she felt she never earned. Instead of dismissing her feelings or defending my colleague, I assured her and her mother that I would speak with the teacher since they were uncomfortable doing so. I reminded the student of her strengths, her hard work, and all the bright qualities I had personally witnessed. In that moment, she felt seen, heard, and affirmed.

What she didn't know was that the real issue began when the principal promoted her to the next grade without consulting the teachers. Her teacher's frustration, meant for the principal, had quietly landed on the child, who internalized it as proof she wasn't enough.

Moments like this remind us why coping skills matter. They don't just calm a storm; they help a young person reclaim their voice. When a child finds that voice again, the world around them shifts just enough for healing to begin.

*Loneliness, Isolation, & Not Finding Their Tribe

- Not having anyone who understands, listens, or relates
- Loneliness, depression, and low mood
- Not finding their tribe leading to a sense of isolation
- Having no place to safely be themselves or express themselves
- Low self-esteem
- Lack of resources or groups for connection to support

Youth and teens have a deep desire to find their tribe. Sometimes it can be difficult to find among their peers, and that is why this work is so important. You are not only a safe adult, a safe place for young people to express what they are feeling, but you are helping them cope with the loneliness and isolation that can be very detrimental in the Arctic. Remember to celebrate your wins as a Behavioral Health Specialist, Foster Care Worker, educator, etc. Every day you show up to work is a chance for you to connect with someone and impact their lives.

Finally Free
By Norman Riggs

The little bird wanted to soar high spreading its wings.
Feeling free, just afraid to leap.
Content sitting in that nested tree.
Watching others soar effortlessly and graciously,
but his fear ran too deep
so that little bird was still content sitting in that nested tree.

As time passed, the little bird decided again to leap.
The distance traveled was more than several feet.
Realizing he too could soar effortlessly and graciously,
he never returned to that nested tree.
That scared little bird was soaring and finally free.

Alaskan Indoor Wellness Activities

Cultural, Community & Relational Practices

- Listening & talking circles facilitated by a traditional healer, BHA, or trained cultural facilitator; creates safe, non-judgmental space for personal sharing and community healing.
- Cultural debriefings
- Family nights & community gatherings
- Singing, dancing, games, competitions, ceremonies, women's house & men's house (feasts, potlatches).
- Traditional talk therapies
- Mentorship programs with elders or skilled community teachers

Group Craft & Creative Activities

- Weaving, carving, painting
- Beading, sewing, basket making
- Leather tanning, regalia making, building functional cultural items
- Communal art activities: drumming, songs, dance, ceremony
  - These connect people to land, mentors, culture, ancestors, and spiritual identity.
  - Provide a safe space to discuss emerging or taboo topics.
  - Build confidence, purpose, and emotional regulation.

Creative, Social & Learning Activities

- Artistic activities (any medium)
- Storytelling of any kind
- Grass weaving
- Potlucks with elders
- Tea parties
- Bible study
- Book clubs
- Card games
- Verbal games like "Two Truths and a Lie"
- Discussions about:
  - Past events
  - Planets/astronomy
  - Dreams & visions
  - Jokes/humor

Traditional, Clinical & Healing Practices

- Massage, bone-setting, acupuncture (Native/Tribal Health clinics)
- Energy work such as reflexology
- Ceremonial practices — steam bath/sweat lodge, fasting, journeys, cleansing, blessings
- Specialized traditional therapies (e.g., cryotherapy)
- One-on-one traditional healing from a trained healer
- Individual support from a Behavioral Health Specialist

Personal Wellness & Self-Care

- Soaking feet
- Washing hair
- Putting on makeup
- Polishing fingernails
- Taking personal time out
- Reviewing past photos
- Writing affirmations
- Envisioning one's future self
- Journaling or reflective writing

Independent Creative Activities

- Writing poetry
- Drawing or sketching
- Crafting small beadwork/sewing pieces
- Baking from scratch
- Listening to music (jamming, dancing freely)
- Attending AA meetings

Traditional Healing & Spiritual Guidance

- Prayer
- Diverse faith practices
- Spiritual stewardship rooted in reciprocity with the natural world (plants, fish, birds, land/water animals as relatives with rights)
- Herbal healing & salve-making

Alaskan Outdoor Wellness Activities

Outdoor & Seasonal Group Activities

- Canoeing & kayaking
- Mountain climbing / long-distance walking
- Fishing
- Hunting & trapping
- Sharing, preparing, and teaching subsistence foods
- Cultivating natural spaces (community gardens, covered growing)
- Sea and bird-based cultural activities
- Seasonal migration activities (winter/summer villages, whale or caribou migration)
- Coffee-centered community gatherings

Movement, Nature & Land-Based

- Walking (supports emotional, physical, and lymphatic wellbeing)
- Gathering plants, flowers, greens, beach foods, berries, roots alone or with elders/peers
- Breathwork

- **Collaborate with:**
    - Tribal case workers
    - Tribal Council members
    - Office of Children's Service (OCS) Indian Child Welfare Act (ICWA) Specialists
    - OCS State Office Service Array Unit
- **Prioritize services offered through Tribal Health Organizations.**
- **Use cultural substitutes:**
    - Home-based crafting
    - Storytelling via elders or virtual gatherings
    - Local walking paths
    - Household-level food preparation
    - Nature-based reflection, even without formal programs

Inupiaq Seal Hunters **by Don Henry**

Poinsetta
By Melody Evans

I like plants.
The green leaves calm me in a way
nothing else can,
and the fact that I can keep them alive
fills me with pride.
Out of all my plants,
I have a poinsettia,
known as the Christmas plant
for its red leaves in the beginning.
They say don't water it too much,
keep it in a dark place and it'll thrive.
But it's funny cuz' my plant is like me,
I need sunlight and water to survive.
I spent too much time in dark places,
so I refuse to put my plant through it.
And I wasn't familiar with the rules to follow them,
so by the time I knew, I said screw it.
So without knowing,
I kept it in the sunshine
and watered it every other week,
thinking I'm doing the right thing.
The leaves began to turn green
and the plant became more of a tree.
But isn't that like me?
Going against the wave,
the next trend and the latest fashion,
cuz' in my mind, I'm what's happenin'.
Like Rick Ross,
I'm the biggest boss I've seen thus far,
and I didn't get here by blending in.
I stand out.

Set apart.
Different.
I go against the grain.
So now the grain has rips in it,
but that's how God built me.
One day, I went to cut off the dead branches
and there was one that refused to be cut...
so I gave up.
A few weeks later,
a little sprout poked its head out
like it was tryna' grow or something.
Another week passed
and the leaves got bigger and bolder
until they were fully grown.
The branch that appeared to be dead
had life that refused to be cut short.
So when anybody looks at me crazy
for doing my own thing,
I'll point them to my poinsettia,
cuz' if it can thrive
when all odds are against it,
then so can I.

Therapeutic Writing by Harriet Slwooko
(Letter to My Dreams, Goals, Ambitions, and Purpose)

My Dear Harriet;

My oh my, what you have achieved in the past 20 + years. You've found your heart's desire for your people. Thank you for the hard work, steadfast dedication it took… never forget that. I believe you always had it in you. The experiences in life, whether good or bad, helped beyond your comprehension. Little did you know this path would not only help you, but others. Do you remember when your sister "checked you out" when you both finally saw each other? I believe she was amazed. So continue on this journey, remember to write your life's mission statement, and keep it in your heart.

Continue on… always forward!

Sincerely,
HL Joy Slw

II. Addressing Suicidal Risk Through Family Communication

Rock Island Cabin **by Don Henry**

***Trauma Exposure (Personal, Family, or Community)**

- Childhood trauma
- Witnessing suicide of others
- Generational trauma
- Experiences of abuse, neglect, or bullying
- Punished when speaking native language & encouraged to stop
- Sexual abuse
- Elder abuse
- Alcohol and drug use
- Past silent treatment
- Past historical traumatic experience.
    - For example, past teachers, Bureau of Indian Affairs (BIA's) treatment toward students
    - Missionaries forced Alaskan Natives/American Indians to attend churches.
- Cultural differences (native people v. more westernized views)
- Problems finding balance with progression from more traditional ways to new cultural norms
- Parental influence
- Not being open towards others
- Grief/deaths
- Suicide taboo in the Alaskan Native/American Indian culture
- Confusion over spiritual beliefs
- Afraid to be themselves
- Mental, emotional, physical, spiritual isolation
- An internal mistrust of their own abilities or instincts
- Feeling lost within their own culture even despite meeting certain life goals.

The Hidden Crisis of Sexual Violence in Alaska

Suicide ideation cannot be fully understood without confronting the reality of sexual violence. Alaska's rates of sexual assault are nearly twice those of the next highest state, creating a persistent landscape of danger that many community members are forced to navigate daily. For victims who experience incest or sexual violence within their own home, the harm is even more profound. In many Alaskan Native and American Indian communities, young adults cannot simply leave home when they turn eighteen. This means their abusers may retain ongoing access to them, compounding trauma over years rather than moments.

As a Survivor Empowerment Council Member with the Ohio Alliance to End Sexual Violence, this reality is agonizing to witness. Healing is possible, but not without systemic change that protects victims rather than the structures that silence them.

Reducing sexual violence in Alaska requires a complete overhaul of how cases are handled: stronger and safer reporting procedures, independent oversight, tribunal review boards, interagency policy alignment, and consistent data collection by both race and gender. Accountability must extend to every level of the system. In places like Nome, where more than 400 sexual assault cases were left uninvestigated, the absence of justice is not a failure. It is a betrayal.

Addressing these failures is not optional. It is a necessary step toward protecting survivors, restoring trust, and ultimately reducing suicide ideation among youth and adults alike.

Parental Factors That Shape Youth Suicide Risk & Support

1. Overcoming parental stigmas & myths
2. Acceptance vs. Judgement
3. Compassion
4. Co-parenting children who are suicidal
5. Making sure parents have resources they need: emergency numbers, preventative suicide prevention plans, and nonverbal suicide prevention communication tools.

The Raven **by Don Henry**

Reflection
By Janae “Afrodytee” Johnson

My head hangs and gazes,
At rippled reflections
Lily padded feelings,
Frogged expectations
Marbled in skipped realization,
Of 14 reasons to be ok.

How can I live the bad days?

Come here, child.
Listen to my words,
I was once you
That scared little girl,
I was so misunderstood.

To cool for cool kids
I wasn't dripped in
Pink finishes
But Wednesdays were always dreaded.

Silly rabbit,
Tricks on me
Halloween couldn't compare,
To what it feels like being ghosted.

How days go by,
But you are coasting.
Fake smile to numbness
Staring at the reflection,
wondering beyond it.

Baby, I been there.
But I learned resilience.
The capacity to recover quickly
Despite difficulty.
Ain't nothing about you faulty,
You light up the room.

So "switch" your perspective.
No, woah is you.
Be electric in knowing,
There's a spark to you.
That firework,
But no July.
Be reflective in knowing,

You're meant to survive,
and to shine so bright,
even your shadows get jealous.

Commentary for "Reflection" by MoPoetry Phillips

"Reflection" reveals the inner turmoil of a young person wrestling with suicide ideation. This person is staring into their own distorted waters, trying to understand the shape of their hurt. The poem lifts a quiet wish many of our youth carry: the hope that a parent will draw them close and say, "Come here, child… I was once you." They long for connection, for someone who recognizes their fear without dismissing it.

Yet many young people never receive that kind of steady, grounding presence. Instead, some parents unintentionally minimize their child's distress, believing today's struggles couldn't possibly compare to what they faced growing up. Others carry their own quiet grief, wrestling with guilt, denial, or the difficult reality that past or present challenges in the home, including substance use, conflict, or unresolved trauma, may have shaped their child's emotional world. These impacts can linger long after the circumstances themselves have changed. Some parents may need to acknowledge the role they played; while also understanding they are not solely responsible for how their children learn to cope over time. Persistent rumination, or reliving past pain without resolution, can stall healing, but thoughtful reflection can strengthen resilience, insight, and growth.

For Behavioral Health Specialists conducting initial assessments, screening for risk, clarifying concerns, establishing goals, and shaping care plans, it's vital to remember what the poem names with such tenderness: the resilience that keeps a young person alive one more day. Beneath the numbness, beneath the skipped stones of self-doubt, there is still a spark. Hold space for that spark. Name it. Celebrate it. Help youth reclaim the brightness they fear they've lost. Guide them toward the understanding that even in their darkest hours, there is something within them still glowing that is stubborn, electric, and deeply worth protecting.

What are Some of the Parental Stigmas & Myths?

- "If a child talks about suicide, they won't actually do it."
- "This generation is soft and can't handle anything."
- "My child has nothing to be depressed about, because they have everything they need."
- "It's just a phase; they'll grow out of it."
- "Talking about suicide will put the idea in their head."
- "They're only doing this for attention."
- "Kids don't experience real stress; adults have the real problems."
- "Therapy means something is 'wrong' with my child or my parenting."
- "Strong families don't need outside help."
- "If I acknowledge their struggles, I'm encouraging weakness."
- "They wouldn't feel this way if they listened, prayed more, or followed the rules."
- "Mental health issues only happen in other families, not ours."
- "Discipline will fix the behavior."
- "Teens exaggerate. It's hormones, not a crisis."

"As we are combating suicide, remember that parents, guardians, and close family members of those impacted by suicide ideation are going through the grieving cycle…shock, denial, anger, bargaining, depression, reflecting, and accepting. They may cycle through, or go through this repeatedly until grieving, even the possible loss of a child or family member, has stopped." -MoPoetry Phillips

***Alaskan Serenity* by Don Henry**

FACES OF SUICIDE
BY ARTS EQUITY COLLECTIVE

Stephen "Twitch" Boss

Lil Wayne

Marshawn Kneeland

Anthony Bourdain

Breaking the Myth: It's Not "Just a Youth Problem"

It's true that a young person's mind is less developed than an adult's mind which causes them to be more reactionary and impulsive. They may move quickly to more permanent solutions like attempting suicide. However, one thing that is important, especially when talking to parents and guardians, is that you remind them that suicide happens in all age categories. We can't blame youth or teens and stereotype them as being overly sensitive or weak.

The "Faces of Suicide" shown on the last page are Robin Williams, Marshawn Kneeland; Stephen "Twitch" Boss, Lil Wayne, and Anthony Bourdain. Although Lil Wayne is still living, he shot himself in the chest at 12 years old which almost cost him his life. Robin Williams was a well-known actor and comedian. He starred in the show, Mork and Mindy, and movies like Good Morning Vietnam and Dead Poets Society. Williams faced depression and in years past he went through alcohol and cocaine abuse. He died by suicide at age 63. Dallas Cowboy, Marshawn Kneeland died by self-inflicted gunshot on November 6, 2025.

We say died by instead of completing or committing suicide, which implies that there was a crime, like hearing the words "commit robbery." Stephen "Twitch" Boss was Ellen DeGeneres' DJ, and he completed suicide at age 40. Today.com stated that he suffered from "high functioning depression." His death shocked the nation and even his wife stated she never saw it coming. Anthony Bourdain died on June 8, 2018, at age 61. He was a celebrity chef, travel show host, and a New York Times bestselling author. Anthony previously recovered from a heroin addiction, but he openly discussed his continued struggles with depression.

His mother said, "He is absolutely the last person in the world I would have ever dreamed would do something like this. He had everything." Suicidal ideation impacts people of all ages, and we must take action to prevent suicide.

Also, as we are combating suicide, remember that parents, guardians, and close family members of those impacted by suicide ideation are going through the grieving cycle below: shock, denial, anger, bargain, depression, reflect, and accept. It's a cycle that is not linear, meaning it doesn't start at #1, shock and end with #7, acceptance. Their emotions and feelings may jump all over the entire diagram. They may cycle through, or go through this repeatedly until grieving, even the possible loss of a child or family member has stopped.

The Things That Still Make Me Smile
By Ramica Babers- BluPoetry

Some days, joy feels like a stranger.
It knocks softly,
unsure if it's still welcome.

But I let it in anyway.
Even when grief sits heavy at the table,
joy still brings light for both of us.

I smile for the random
kindness of strangers,
for playlists that understand heartbreak,
for the smell of rain that reminds me
how cleansing feels.

I smile in the mirror,
even when it looks tired of
seeing me survive.
For the breath, I almost gave up on
that still shows up without being asked.

I smile for the child I was-
the one who thought love had left for good.
For the teen who thought nobody noticed.
For the grown-up who still gets nervous
but speaks anyway.

I smile for the small things:
the way sunlight sneaks through closed blinds,
the way laughter finds its way back home.
For every scar that learned to shimmer
instead of sting.

See, this smile?
It's not decoration-
Its declaration.
A promise to keep showing up,
even when joy arrives late.

So, if your mouth forgot how,
borrow mine.
You can hold it
until yours remembers.

***Umiaq Hunters* by Don Henry**

Fighting the Current: Acceptance Over Judgment

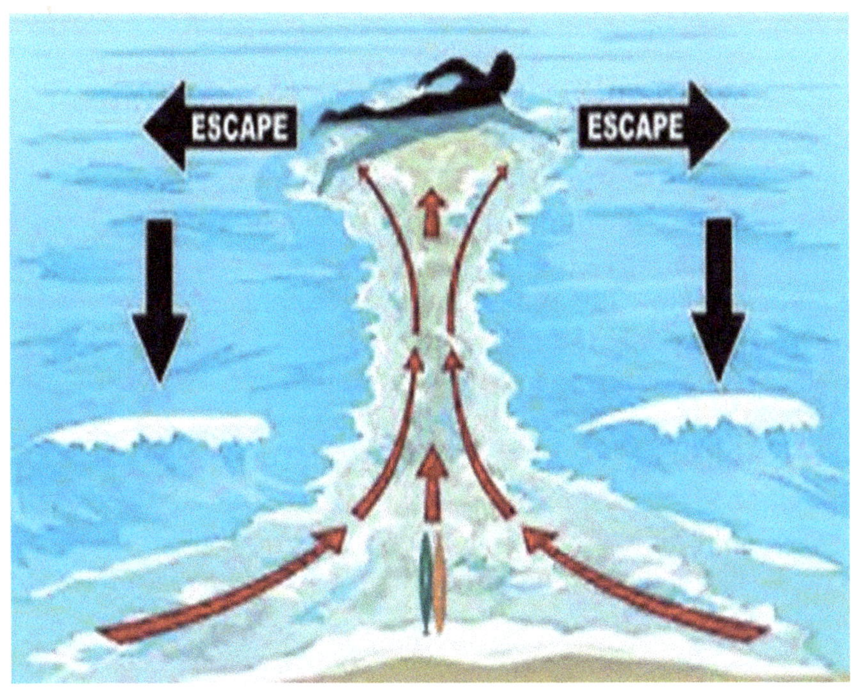

When looking at acceptance, I like to use the image above. The man is attempting to swim despite being caught up in the current within the water, and he is in extreme danger even if he is an expert swimmer. The current fights to pull him down, sweep him under, and cause him to drown. Many youths and teens who are suicidal don't want to die. They want to end the current version of their life. Understand that our youth are fighting hard against the current. Today, the current is as strong as it has ever been.

As suicide prevention advocates help parents, caregivers, even churches learn acceptance over judgment. Acceptance is acknowledging that there is a problem. Judgment is projecting your individual experiences, feelings, or beliefs onto the child. When you are judgmental, you are minimizing the child's thoughts and feelings. We all need to accept when a child is battling with suicide ideation. Failing to do so will isolate the child, cause them to feel they can't confide in you and tell their feelings, and may push them to die by suicide.

Trigger Warning
By Jodie L. Summers

And it comes in waves...
Torrential downpours of terrifying things, crashing against this barrier,
This structure, the safe place I thought I built.
Wave after wave crashing against the sanity I escaped into,
crumbling and eroding away the impenetrability I thought I once had.
Revealing cracks in foundations I left too long
and thought I could cover up with something distracting.
And it comes when you become too confident...
Drawing you in deeper to your triggers and trauma that you once knew how to deal with,
stripping away coping mechanisms and leaving you in a panic state,
but knowing if you gasp for air, you'll drown.
So, you hold on tighter to that last burning breath, struggling to reach the surface,
because a whisper could kill you and all you want to do is be loud,
as you reach to break the surface of what has dragged you beneath its influence.
And it comes when things are calm...
You see the still waters and think that just beneath the surface
there might be something worth reaching for.
The treasures that others say they've found by diving deep within themselves
and pulling out miracles, but every time you go in you get bit and lose another part of
yourself trying to struggle through this endless sea of inconsistency.
They find dolphins where you find sharks,
while you were busy surviving through your traumas and nightmares
that you grew up to fight, they had imaginary friends and consistent circles of people
to protect them their whole life.
And it comes in waves...
Pulling you closer to the edge of insanity, tearing away the fragile layers of reality
that shape up your identity as you watch people who were once very close and held
strong ties to the shores you believed you could live on forever,
suddenly disappear and let you drift further away.
Sometimes it's a smell, a place, name, photo or even a song that may play in your mind as
you reminisce about the memories that take you down these tidal waves of isolation and
leave you contemplating if you should just let the current take you away...
While the sea might be full of fish, there's only one you,
only one living being on this planet that you have to be honest with and accept
accountability for all actions you take, when these uncontrollable tsunamis try and wreck
your life.
And it comes...
When you've held that smile too long, knowing you deserve to cry, let out all of those
unpack things that you no longer need to let hold weight on your soul and breathe.

The Power of Compassion in Preventing Suicide

Once parents and caregivers begin to practice acceptance, the next essential step is compassion. Compassion is a suicide prevention lifeline. When adults assume a child is "just seeking attention," they risk dismissing real danger. They must understand that no sign of suicide ideation can be brushed aside. And under no circumstance should anyone tell a young person to "go ahead and do it" as a way to call their bluff; that kind of response can be catastrophic.

It also helps to gently guide parents away from the familiar "When I was your age…" speeches. These comparisons rarely build connection. Childhood pressures have always existed, but today's young people navigate an amplified world: online visibility, academic demands, social pressure, and a constant stream of judgment that never turns off. Their pain isn't less valid, because it doesn't resemble what adults experienced years ago.

Caregivers may struggle with resentment when crisis interrupts the flow of daily life. Supporting a child through suicide ideation often requires rearranging schedules, missing work, pausing social plans, and stepping out of familiar routines. Encourage parents to acknowledge and accept these sacrifices in order to be present.

Finally, compassion includes accepting uncertainty. When a child says, "I don't know what's wrong, but I don't feel right," the goal is not to demand clarity they don't have. Many of us have felt unnamed heaviness at some point in our lives. Instead of insisting on explanations, parents can offer calm presence, patience, and an open door. With time, understanding often arrives, and communication can deepen.

Co-parenting Children Who are Suicidal

Supporting a suicidal child is not a solo mission. It is a shared responsibility across the entire family system. Co-parenting happens whether caregivers live in the same home or separate ones, and it can include grandparents, relatives, or any trusted adult in the child's circle.

1. Build a Unified Support Team

- Love, protection, and emotional care must come from every adult involved, not just one.
- Each caregiver may be at a different level of acceptance. One may fully acknowledge the child's suicidal thoughts while another is still in denial. This mismatch is common, and it takes time to align.

2. Work Toward One Accord

- Even if acceptance levels differ, all adults must commit to working together to reduce suicidal ideation.
- Invite every caregiver, including extended family, if possible, into counseling sessions or meetings with clinicians.
- Give extra copies of safety plans or educational materials and share them with everyone responsible for the child's care.

3. Protect the Child from Adult Conflict

- Encourage parents/caregivers to discuss disagreements privately, never in front of the child.
- When a child sees caregivers arguing because of them, they may feel like a burden. This can deepen despair and increase risk.

4. Prepare for Outside Influences

- Even if the primary caregivers are aligned, other family members or trusted adults may not agree with the plan or may minimize the child's struggles.
- Acknowledge this possibility and prepare caregivers to respond calmly. A single dismissive comment from a relative, friend, or neighbor can deeply wound a child already battling suicidal thoughts.

Making Sure Parents Have Resources They Need

1. Emergency numbers
2. Preventative Suicide Prevention Plans
3. Nonverbal Suicide Prevention Communication Tools

As part of the K.C. Suicide Prevention Plan, we have all participants take out their phones and save the necessary suicide prevention hotline phone numbers. We strongly encourage everyone to adopt this method. It's better to have it and not need it, than need it and not have it.

NAMI
National Alliance on Mental Illness
MENTAL HEALTH
RESOURCES
for the
Indigenous/Native
American Community

988 Suicide & Crisis Lifeline – Indigenous Support

Phone: 988 (24/7, free, confidential)
Website: 988lifeline.org

The 988 Lifeline offers immediate crisis support, with a dedicated portal for American Indian, Alaska Native, and Indigenous individuals. Services include suicide prevention, emotional support, and crisis intervention.

We R Native

Website: wernative.org

A comprehensive health and wellness resource for Native youth. Features culturally relevant content on mental health, suicide prevention, relationships, community support, identity, and healthy lifestyles.

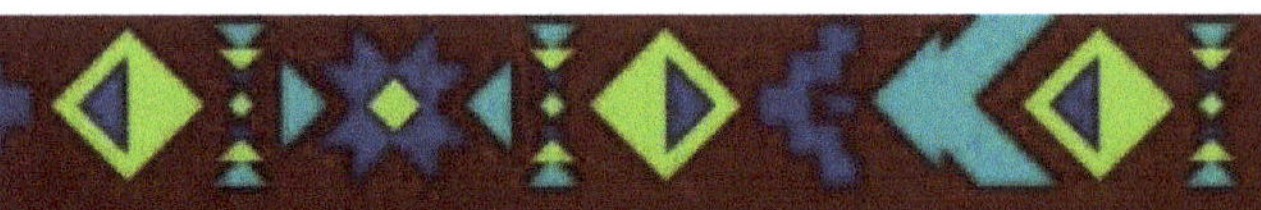

Suicide Prevention Resource Center (SPRC) – AI/AN Focus

Website: sprc.org

Provides guidance, toolkits, and best practices specifically developed for American Indian and Alaska Native communities. Focus areas include suicide prevention, postvention, and community-level prevention strategies.

NICOA – National Council on Indian Aging

Phone: 505-292-2001
Website: Nicoa.org

A national nonprofit focused on the needs of aging American Indian and Alaska Native elders, linking elders to culturally competent care, educational information, federal resources, and more.

National Indigenous Women's Resource Center (NIWRC)

Website: niwrc.org

Provides national leadership, culturally specific training, and policy advocacy to protect Indigenous women, families, and communities. Offers resources on trauma, healing, safety, and community capacity building

Indian Health Service (IHS) – Behavioral Health

Website: **ihs.gov/mentalhealth**

Provides comprehensive behavioral health services throughout Tribal communities. The IHS Behavioral Health Program includes resources for trauma, suicide prevention, substance use, crisis response, and community healing.

Indian Country Child Trauma Center

Phone:(405) 271-8858

The Indian Country Child Trauma Center provides essential training, resources, and program support for trauma-informed care tailored to tribal communities. Through specialized technical assistance and program development, this center helps strengthen healing pathways for children and families in Indian Country.

One Sky Center

e-Mail: onesky@ohsu.edu
Website: ihs.gov/mentalhealth

A national resource center providing resources and a "Find a Therapist" locator for treating mental health and substance use disorder within Native American communities.

StrongHearts Native Helpline

Phone: 1-844-7NATIVE (1-844-762-8483)
Website: strongheartshelpline.org

A safe, confidential, and culturally grounded helpline staffed by Native advocates. Support includes crisis counseling, safety planning, domestic violence guidance, dating violence, sexual assault services, and referrals to local Tribal programs.
Text and online chat available 24/7.

Crisis Text Line – Native/Indigenous Keyword

Text: NATIVE to 741741
(24/7 access to trained crisis counselors)

Provides immediate, text-based confidential support for Native/Indigenous individuals

Do You Need Encouraging Words? – Text "Caring" to 65664. You will receive two texts per week containing encouraging messages, funny videos, and songs to boost your mood.

Need to Speak with Someone? - Help is just a text away as well. Make sure clients, parents, and guardians know that when in crisis they can text number "741741" for the Crisis Text Line. This is a free, 24/7 service that provides confidential support. To connect with a trained volunteer counselor text "HOME" for help with anxiety, depression, bullying, or suicidal thoughts.

What if you are a college student in need of help? Texting "COLLEGE" to 65664 provides Native American college students access to We R Native's College Caring Messages of encouragement and tips from other students to support their well-being and success in college.

The next two letters attack grief from two opposing angles. The first, by Renetta Hobson looks at the grief that is felt before a person has passed on. Although they are with you, the pain is still very real. The second letter by Tareze Grant addresses both grief and loss. Writing through both experiences allows clients to express. Tareze used Prompt: 2: Letter to Someone Who is No Longer in Your Life (Deceased, Divorced, Breakup, Friendship Ended/Someone who Abandoned or Betrayed you).

Therapeutic Letter Writing by Renetta Hobson

Dear Grandma/ "MaDear;"

You are the wind beneath my wings.
Your words, wisdom and wit shine through
for all who are blessed by your presence.

Your faith built the foundation for our family.
Your vision charted the path for legacy.

Your strength gives us hope.
Your focus has aways been family.
Your grit and determination inspire me daily.
Your skills and focus have kept us together.

I accept that you are getting frail.
I accept that time will bring about a change in the family.
I accept that sometimes your memory faulters.
I accept that one day the family will hold you in our memory.

Love,
Renetta

Therapeutic Letter Writing by Tareze Grant

Dear Grandma;

I'm writing this letter from Kotzebue, Alaska. Yes, Ma'am, I said Alaska. I can hear your voice now saying, "Get out that cold weather before you catch a cold!" You always had big expectations for me, and I am trying to live up to those expectations. It hurt me when you left me on my senior prom day which coincidentally landed on April Fool's Day, but this was absolutely not a joke. You never got the chance to see me dressed in my tuxedo with my prom date or take pictures with me. I was broken that you were no longer with us. Though I thought I lost you that morning, you found a way to save my life that night. After prom, I was about to accept an invitation to an after party. I thought about going and drinking or doing drugs to take the pain away. As I went to press send, I heard a familiar voice say, "Don't go." The voice was yours that I thought was no longer with me. I believe you saved my life that night, and I thank God for you. It's funny how life works from living behind your house eight years ago in Mississippi to living in Alaska just a little over three months. You'll always be a part of my life and in my heart. I miss you! But I am grateful for the time and years I was able to experience with you. I am thankful you saved my life, so that I can be here today making you proud. I still have my first check waiting on you as you joked was yours when I got my first job. It hurts less now. From hyperventilating and crying in my college dorm room on your death date to now being able to cope with it, I know you're proud. You've seen the struggles and successes, but I will continue to make you proud. I will stay warm here in Alaska.

*Mental Health Stigmas & Cultural Barriers

- Mental health stigma in families, communities, and villages, especially Alaskan Native, American Indian, and African American communities.
- Being raised to believe that "What goes on in this house, stays in this house."
- Dismissing depression, and anxiety as attitude or drama.
- Families rejecting therapy, because "Jesus will fix it."
- Belief that faith alone should solve mental health struggles
- Cultural influences (past and present) contributing to family separation
- Feeling like they are living in two worlds (western/modern) and traditional
- Guilt from their current views conflicting with traditional values
- Struggling with integration and the pressure to fit in
- Current silent treatment
- Judgement from peers
- Overthinking about their own lives
- Everyone knows everyone
- Fear of judgment
- Belief that mental health issues are a sign of weakness
- Isolation
- Feeling unaccepted
- Being seen only from one viewpoint
- Not being able to express their full self

Paper Thin
By Lisa Marie Ashby

I had become a patchwork of paper skin
bandaged folded and taped like the edges of packages
healing isn't the same as hiding
licking wounds in silence
unaddressed and pressed in our upper corners
enveloped inwards
even paper cranes desire to migrate away
I used to tear myself at the edges
bent back to the quick
trying to see where I ended
every rip was proof I still had shape
skin is more silent than paper
it doesn't scream when it splits
but the scars don't tell the stories
they only bind them in
the thinnest sheet of paper can hold the weight of wounded words
but silence can fold you into yourself
smaller each day
crease by careful crease
trying to turn pain into symmetry
micro traumas reopening the past up
stinging like paper cuts
ripping pages of myself out
entire passages missing
where I should have just written
I'm hurting
healing isn't the same as hiding
so I'm ironing all the crinkles out
the pages that I crumpled up
are no longer ruined
unfolded and scarred
like lace snowflakes

I am made of paper skin
no longer folded from within
but written with intention
an anthology of phantom chapters and reclaimed ink
where the torn-out parts
have been rendered as wings
and the silence that once bound me
becomes the sound of my future unfolding.

***Umiaq Travelers* by Don Henry**

Avoiding Toxic Positivity in Suicide Prevention

Avoiding toxic positivity means acknowledging a child's pain instead of minimizing it with phrases like "stay positive" or "you'll be fine." When a child is experiencing suicidal ideation, they need validation, active listening, and emotional presence, not forced optimism. Creating space for their real feelings builds trust, safety, and a pathway toward genuine support and healing.

Youth Expression Matters: Moving Beyond Labels and Assumptions

As an educator or someone working with youth, it is easy to dismiss depression, and anxiety as attitude or drama. First, there has been a cultural shift in how youth worldwide communicate with their elders. There was a generation where youth were supposed to be seen but not heard. There were distinct parental and child roles that restricted children from giving input, saying how they feel, and showing that they were impacted by anything going on within the family, or the household. Even today, especially in multigenerational households where youth and teens are raised by their grandparents, you may still see these rules being imposed on the child. However, due to television, movies, and social media, youth living in rural Alaska are learning to communicate differently with their peers and families. Generational differences can cause us, as adults (both parents and educators) to be biased, unsympathetic to how children express their emotions, or display toxic positivity.

Secondly, we can quickly give out labels based on their behavior instead of asking ourselves if what the child is displaying is the result of current or past trauma. When is the last time you've asked yourself if a child is safe at home, or if they have enough to eat? There are so many factors that impact our daily interaction with them.

Lastly, understand that the shift you see with our youth is necessary. They aren't just youth and teens; they are human beings with feelings. They can't heal in silence. It is up to us to build trust and create a safe space where they can speak their truth, articulate their pain, and convey their needs. Caseworkers have done casework long enough. It is time to do inner work: seeing the individual child and supporting them as they work through inner turmoil.

As you look at "C-PTSD: the Four 'Stress' Responses, think about the one client on your caseload, student in your class, or residential placement center that is truly an atmosphere shifter. When they show up for group or class feeling down, it seems to impact the entire room. It causes you to struggle to keep them from high jacking the entire group facilitation or lesson plan with off-topic conversations, aggression towards others around them, complaints about engaging, or flat-out refusal to engage. Despite redirecting, de-escalation, and all the other textbook and on-the-job skills you've learned to use, at the end of the day you feel exhausted. Things didn't go as planned.

After you've had time to breathe and decompress, reconsider what you've experienced. Instead of an outburst, has the child seen fighting, been physically, sexually, or emotionally abused and now they are having a fight trauma response? Are they disengaged, refusing to remove bulky clothing, hats or hoods, because they have been sexually abused and the traumatic event has caused them to freeze, desire to be hidden, and despise being touched? Are they hypersexualized and starving for attention? Whether or not the behavior is a manifestation of trauma from sexual abuse has to be considered, because when tracking sexual violence in Alaska among Alaskan Native and Native Americans the Center for Disease Control says 58% of women and 51% of men experienced intimate partner violence during their lifetime. The first step to working in areas of youth suicide prevention is to increase your sensitivity, empathy, understanding of childhood trauma of various types, and how children in distress respond.

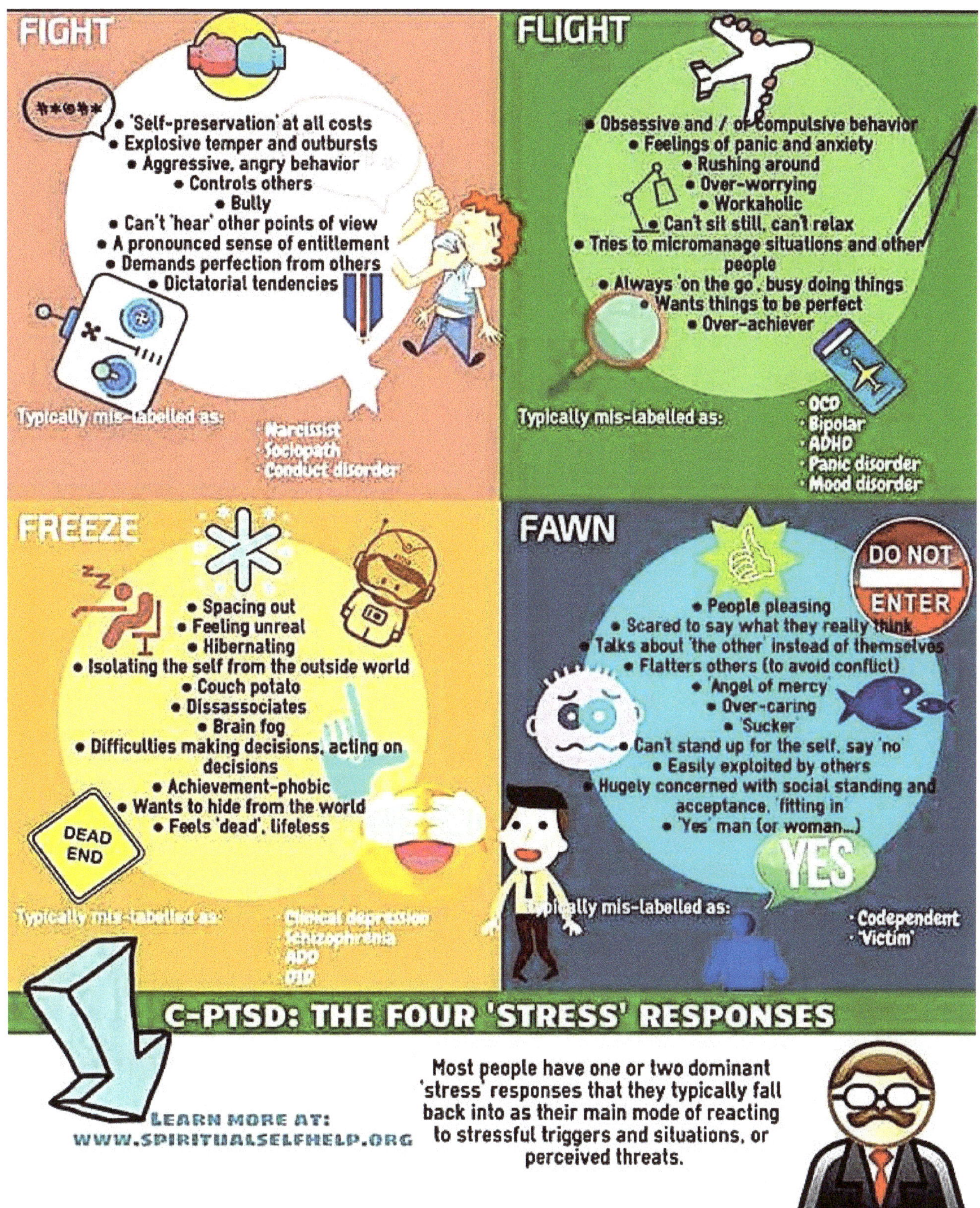

FIGHT
• 'Self-preservation' at all costs
• Explosive temper and outbursts
• Aggressive, angry behavior
• Controls others
• Bully
• Can't 'hear' other points of view
• A pronounced sense of entitlement
• Demands perfection from others
• Dictatorial tendencies
Typically mis-labelled as:
· Narcissist
· Sociopath
· Conduct disorder
FLIGHT
• Obsessive and / or compulsive behavior
• Feelings of panic and anxiety
• Rushing around
• Over-worrying
• Workaholic
• Can't sit still, can't relax
• Tries to micromanage situations and other people
• Always 'on the go', busy doing things
• Wants things to be perfect
• Over-achiever
Typically mis-labelled as:
· OCD
· Bipolar
· ADHD
· Panic disorder
· Mood disorder
FREEZE
• Spacing out
• Feeling unreal
• Hibernating
• Isolating the self from the outside world
• Couch potato
• Dissassociates
• Brain fog
• Difficulties making decisions, acting on decisions
• Achievement-phobic
• Wants to hide from the world
• Feels 'dead', lifeless
DEAD END
Typically mis-labelled as:
Clinical depression
Schizophrenia
ADD
DID
FAWN
DO NOT ENTER
• People pleasing
• Scared to say what they really think
• Talks about 'the other' instead of themselves
• Flatters others (to avoid conflict)
• 'Angel of mercy'
• Over-caring
• 'Sucker'
• Can't stand up for the self, say 'no'
• Easily exploited by others
• Hugely concerned with social standing and acceptance, 'fitting in'
• 'Yes' man (or woman...)
YES
Typically mis-labelled as:
· Codependent
· 'Victim'
C-PTSD: THE FOUR 'STRESS' RESPONSES
LEARN MORE AT:
WWW.SPIRITUALSELFHELP.ORG
Most people have one or two dominant 'stress' responses that they typically fall back into as their main mode of reacting to stressful triggers and situations, or perceived threats.

Anxiety Scale

1	**Minimal**	• Small feelings of worry/anxiety. • Able to get things done and focus on tasks. • Little to no physical symptoms.
2	**Mild**	• Anxious throughout the day but not all day. • Some changes in concentration and sleep. • Stomach ache and muscle tension.
3	**Moderate**	• Anxious most of the day. • Changes in sleep, appetite, concentration. • Avoidance. • Feeling panicky, headaches, and fatigue.
4	**Severe**	• Anxiety all day. • Feeling breathless, chest tightness, digestive issues. • Unable to focus. • Sensory overload. • Isolation.
5	**Debilitating** I TheMindsJournal	• Severe anxiety all day. • Panic attacks. • Can't function. • Intense physical symptoms. • Feeling paralyzed. • Meltdowns. • Obsessive thoughts. • Feeling unable to continue.

MINDJOURNAL

Letter to My Past Trauma: I Don't Know If I Can Just Mention Your Name, Past Trama by Dollie A.K. Hawley

Dear Miss Dollie H.K. Hawley's Past Life;

Well! It's hard to think or bring back my past life, but I just have to write you this letter. Just thinking about my past brings joy, peace, happiness, and such great harmony. But part of my thoughts brings me back to unworthy thoughts. I think thoughts will never go away. I know that on the other side of my past life there stands a door that is completely shut. When I look at it, I want it to remain shut and completely locked for good, because I don't feel that I deserved to be treated that way. Growing up as a little girl, I felt the world I lived in was unpredictable. My past stuck to me like Gorilla Glue whether I liked it or not. My past gave me a sense of hope and direction. Yet sometimes I felt stuck there, but by the grace of God or fate. Life will make a move to bring my past life to bloom once again. Maybe, my past hurt, pain, and baggage will allow me to bloom like a Forget-Me-Not Flower. Like a colorful butterfly who spread its wings upon the universe. My past is unknown to the soul and spirit of my life, but maybe I still should not open this past door of mine. Whether I like it or not, only God or fate knows the answer to what unfolds before me. Just learn to live in the moment.

Safety Plan- by Arts Equity Collective's K.C. Suicide Prevention Program (pg.1)

DEPRESSION- Depression causes low mood and decreased interest in doing things that used to be fun. Depression is considered an illness when the symptoms do not go away and make it very difficult to do usual activities. Depression is a treatable illness. This plan will help you and your team work together to make you better.

SELF-CARE: Taking good care of yourself is the first step to getting better. Think about how you are doing and in which areas you would like to improve. Pick 1-2 to work on first.

SLEEP - An average of 8 hours of sleep a night is ideal for most teens. Avoiding screens/light/TV for 30 minutes before bed makes it easier for your body to fall asleep.

EXERCISE - Exercise releases natural hormones called endorphins that help improve your mood. Work up to regular exercise every day.

NUTRITION - Three meals with a good variety of foods based on your age and activity level will help you maintain a good energy level and get the nutrients you need. Visit www.choosemyplate.gov for more information.

SCHEDULE TIME WITH OTHERS - Plan something fun to do in person with someone else. Spending time with loved ones improves happiness.

DO SOMETHING YOU ENJOY - Hobbies help us relax and improve mood.

SPIRITUAL/RELAXATION - Discuss with family members how they have used spiritual tools, prayer, meditation or relaxation techniques to help them in their lives. If you wish, develop a plan that works for you.

THERAPY: For most teens, the next part of the treatment plan is therapy. Many types of therapy have been found to be useful. Most therapists are trained in different types of therapy, and they will work for you to determine the type that will be most effective. A good relationship with your therapist is important.

MEDICATION: Some patients may benefit from medication in addition to or instead of therapy. Your medical provider and therapist will work with you to decide if this is best.

Safety Plan- by Arts Equity Collective's K.C. Suicide Prevention Program (pg.2)

SAFETY PLAN

My main goal. (How will I know I'm better?)

____

____

Top (3) trusted adults:

1.

____

2.

____

3.

____

My self-care goals:

1.

____

2.

____

3.

____

My Therapist:

____

My Primary Care Physician:

____

Safety Plan- by Arts Equity Collective's K.C. Suicide Prevention Program (pg.3)

Family:

____

____

Other Trusted Adult:

____

Signed: ____ **Date:** ___________

Witness: ____ **Date:** ___________

Safety Plan- by Arts Equity Collective's K.C. Suicide Prevention Program (pg.4)

NOTES:

Creating Nonverbal Communication Suicide Prevention Tools

When my son was receiving counseling after a suicide attempt, his therapist asked whether he felt safe keeping his bedroom door open or closed. Despite clearly understanding the question, he could not bring himself to answer. In that moment, I realized something many families face: even when surrounded by love, some children simply cannot put their pain into words. Arts Equity Collective recognizes that silence is not a lack of feeling, it is often a symptom of overwhelming internal struggle, including suicidal ideation.

To offer families an added layer of protection, we created the K.C. Nonverbal Communication Suicide Prevention Tool, featured on the previous page. This tool empowers youth to communicate their emotional state without needing to speak which is an essential option for those who shut down verbally during crisis. As Behavioral Health Specialists, foster care workers, educators, and parents, we ask you to help youth create and use these tools daily. They are simple yet lifesaving. Green indicates they are feeling well, yellow signals they need support or increased awareness, and red alerts caregivers that the child is experiencing suicidal thoughts and needs immediate attention. This activity can be done using 8x3.23Inch PVC Doorknob Hangers Blank Door Signs purchased on Amazon.com, or DIY Spinning Cards Crafts Kit, Coloring Your Own Spinning Paper DIY Colored Blank Wheel Cards for Handmade Classes Party Craft Toys Supplies purchased on Walmart.com.

The Parent and Student Pledges on the next page outline how each person plays a role in maintaining honesty, safety, and connection. Together, we can give young people a voice, even when their voice cannot speak.

K. C. Suicidal Prevention Pledge Agreement

Student's Pledge

I ____agree to offer my family extra security and help those who love me better communicate with me by using the K.C Nonverbal Communication Suicide Prevention Tool throughout the day to help communicate with my family even when I can't say verbally that I am in need, hurting, or feel suicidal. Each morning, I will do a mental health check-in with myself. If I am feeling ok, I will select green. If I feel concerned, or that something isn't right, even if I can't explain what it is, I agree to display yellow. If at any time, I am feeling suicidal, or having thoughts of suicide, I will display red to signal for help. I agree to update this prevention tool anytime my mood changes and continue to do self-check-ins to gauge how I am feeling. Sign your name below if you agree to use this.

____

Student's Name

Parents' Pledge

I ____, agree to be a proactive, not just a reactive parent. I want to know that my child has a way to communicate with me even when they can't verbally say they need me. I agree to work with my child to incorporate the use of this tool daily. I agree to make it a point to check in several times a day to see what color my child has selected. I understand that green means everything is ok. If my child ever chooses yellow, I will use the skills I've learned in the workshop, to communicate verbally with my child and pay close attention to any further change(s) in the color selected. I agree that if my child is ever on red, I will take my child to the nearest Hospital Emergency room for further evaluation while remaining loving, present, and calm. Please sign your name below if you agree with the pledge

____

Name of Parent or Guardian

____

Name of Parent or Guardian

III. Addressing Suicide Through Technology Awareness

Before we address youth and teen social media use, as suicide prevention advocates and workers ask yourself these questions:

1. Do you use social media?
2. If so, why do you use social media?
3. What is the longest social media rabbit hole you have been down?

Why Do Teens Use Social Media

- Escape from the real world
- Avoid facing their problems
- It provides immediate gratification and praise in the form of likes and comments

According to Pew Research Center's, "Teens, Social Media and Technology 2023," about 90% of U.S. teens (ages 13–17) say they use **YouTube**, the most popular platform.

For other major platforms: around 63% use **TikTok**, 61% use **Instagram**, and 55% use **Snapchat**.

Daily and near-constant use is also high: about 73% of teens report visiting **YouTube** daily.

What this means in practice: Given that the U.S. teenage population (13–17) is roughly 16–18 million (depending on the year), the data suggests that well over 10 million U.S. teens are active on social media every day.

Subscribe
By Jodie L. Summers

What happened to people,
where did we go.
We don't have conversations anymore—
everything is a trauma bond
or triggering in some way.
I used to go to my friend's page
and see something that happened in their day,
and now all I see
are short clips from other people’s lives.
I don't know if you, are even you anymore,
because I don't see you no more
just advertisements
and triggering information
I really did not need to know.
But now, I'm staring at it in awe
because that could be me.
It's like people don't even read the terms of service anymore
just click and instantly apply this filter
to whatever might be happening in your real life,
so someone will respond to you,
and the algorithm will let more of the friends
you already have
see what you're doing.
But if that many people responded to you in person,
all at once,
you would be terrified.
Overwhelmed by the sight
every waking moment.
I feel lost
in the connections of others,
numb and overstimulated
at the same time.

But I just received a notification
that my viewership is down,
and if I applied this many filters,
boosted this post,
or bought this check
that unlocks exclusive opportunities,
and posted this many short clips
of people abusing all of humanity
while my head floats in the corner,
desensitized to chat…
(Funny story: when I first started streaming,
I thought "chat" was a person named Tom
who was always trying to encourage me,
until I found out
it was just the comments.)
I might make a dollar or two
and my rent is due.
Prices have gone up,
and I vacation only
to take a viral pic or video
that some influencer
who I'm almost 90% sure
might not even be the real them
since AI[3] is the thing now
said I should do
so I can be free.
And the whole time
you're in complete remorse,
cause things don't seem to be getting any better.
Autocorrect is awesome
trying to sound human
I hope you got that line back.

But our ancestors…
the people before we decided
to put ourselves in tiny boxes
and pay bills
and listen to people who look down on us
but ask for all of our wealth—
they didn't have therapists,
didn't have healthcare
(which now feels like a life sentence
into a death you might not be able to afford).
They had nature,
and ancestors,
and long walks,
and breaking bread with each other
villages that relied upon one another,
accountability,
and making mistakes until you get it right.
Not letting some generated program
that stole from other people's
hard-won wisdom make your own empty.
That's what logging on feels like now.
So I ask, what happened to people,
where did we all go?
Sucked into our own devices,
our personal hells,
obsessing over something that gives nothing back
but an empty black hole
ever hungry, lacking compassion
because it has none.
It only imitates what we feed it.
And as we give less and less
to ourselves,
maybe it does
start to look more like
our reality.

*Social Media Pressure & Unrealistic Standards

- Lack of self-worth, feeling they're not enough due to social media
- Constant comparison and perceived inadequacy
- Feeling attacked or defensive due to people only seeing one side
- Being ganged up on for their beliefs
- Cyberbullying
- Seeing unexpected news of death or tragedy

Negative Outcomes from Excessive Social Media in Rural Communities

1. Negatively impacts their real-life relationships

2. Negatively impacts academic achievements

3. Low self-esteem

4. Depression

5. Body issues

6. Social isolation

Scrolling: Youth Presence on Social Media

Alaska's rural landscape creates natural social distance, long winters, extreme cold, geographic isolation, and economic challenges which all limit connection. Because of this, it's especially important to pay attention to the influence of social media on our teens. Instead of helping them connect, it often pulls them further away from real-life interaction. The result can be deep loneliness, emotional withdrawal, and growing mental-health concerns.

Before we focus on teens, think back to our earlier conversation about why we use social media as adults: distraction, escape, affirmation, entertainment. Many of those reasons apply to youth as well, but for them the impact is amplified. Social media becomes an escape from real-world stress. It offers a place to hide instead of face problems. For some, it becomes their main source of identity, validation, and belonging.

During our in-person workshops, someone mentioned a "family history of low self-esteem." That struck a chord. Self-esteem shapes how confidently we move through the world, and social media can inflate or shatter it within seconds. Likes and comments create instant gratification, but also instant comparison. This is especially harmful for Alaskan Native and Native American youth who are already navigating intergenerational trauma, cultural pressure, or limited access to mental-health support.

The concern is not hypothetical. There are ongoing class-action lawsuits against Instagram for its documented links to youth suicide ideation. This matters for a simple reason: Instagram is built entirely on images. No long posts, no backstory. Instagram is just pictures, videos, and filters that reshape reality into something polished and unattainable. These unrealistic standards feel harsh. American beauty standards can contribute to eating disorders, food restriction, over-exercise, and body shame. Also, woven through all of this is a theme we cannot ignore: social isolation intensified not by distance alone, but by the illusion of connection that replaces genuine community.

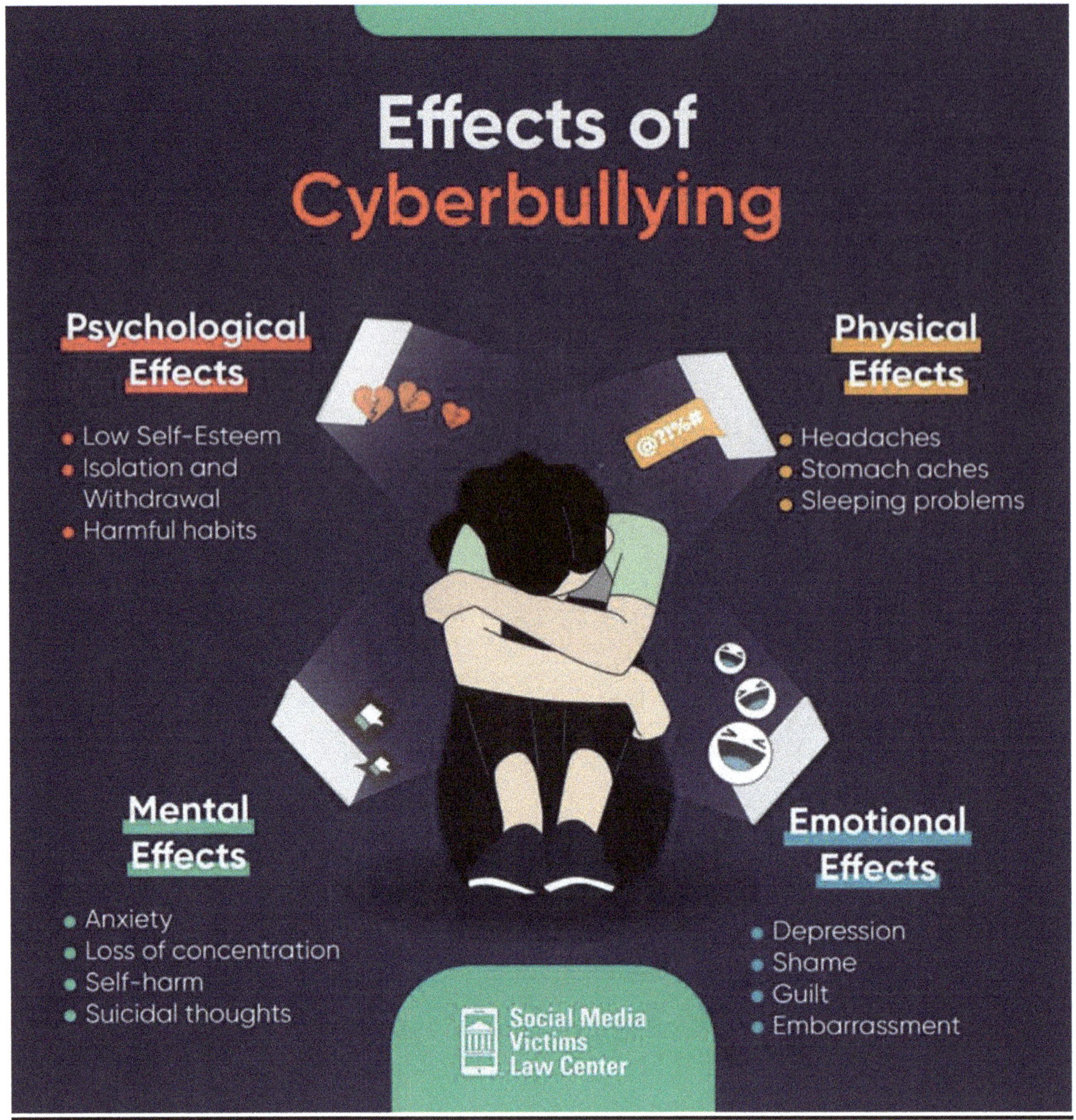

Social media and even gaming are opening up our youth and teens to cyberbullying. Cyberbullying can come in many forms including sending, posting, or sharing negative, harmful, false, or mean content about someone else. This hurts them emotionally and mentally which can lead to depression, feelings of sadness, and loss of interest in activities. It can cause physical problems and fights as well when teens actually see each other face to face. We have to really watch our kids within the LGBTQ+ community. Many of them are being publicly humiliated or outed on social media due to their sexuality. People are coming with receipts: they are posting screenshots of personal conversations, dropping photos, even using photoshop and Artificial Intelligence (AI) to fabricate stories against our youth.

Recognizing Cyberbullying in Youth & Teens

As suicide-prevention workers, it's essential to recognize when a client **is** experiencing or has experienced cyberbullying.

Key indicators Include:

Patterns in Social Media Behavior

- Frequent switching between social media accounts.
- Sudden activation, deactivation, or deletion of accounts.
- Leaving one account and returning under a new name or pseudonym, especially one that is not easily identifiable as them.
- Creating new accounts that disconnect from their old online identity (e.g., new friend lists, no listed birthday, no listed city where they live).

Signs of Digital Avoidance or Reinvention

- Multiple accounts created within a short period of time.
- Accounts with minimal personal information to avoid being found.
- A pattern of withdrawing from online communities where they previously felt comfortable.

Phone-Related Red Flags

- Frequent changes of their phone number.
- Avoiding calls or messages due to harassment.

Best Practices for Suicide-Prevention Workers

- Include social media and cyberbullying questions in routine assessments.
- Ask not only how much time they spend online but also have them show their screen-time data.
- Go beyond "Have you ever been cyberbullied?"
- Ask them confidentially to list all the social media names/usernames they have ever used to identify concerning patterns or hidden accounts.

*Hopelessness & Lack of Future Vision

- Not seeing a future
- Feeling like there's no path forward
- Some youth being very aware of themselves and deciding they don't want to be in the world
- Lack of opportunities: work, education, & career path/development
- Lack of support for connection

IF PAIN &
TRAUMA CAN
BE PASSED
DOWN
THROUGH
GENERATIONS,
THEN SO CAN
HEALING.

@medicine_mami

The Night Be Lying
By Ramica Babers-BluPoetry

The night be lying.
It whispers slick,
like it knows something you don't.
Tell you nobody cares.
Tell you quiet is peace.
Tell you the world doesn't need you anymore.

But hush-
that voice doesn't love you.
It just wants your silence.

I know that space between breaths,
where you ain't trying to disappear,
you just want the hurt to stop echoing.
Where you stare at the ceiling,
counting cracks like exits,
waiting for something-anything-to shift.
I've been there.
Where the dark feels holy
and the light feels too far to reach.
Where you wonder if anybody
would notice if your smile went missing.

But listen, love-
the night be lying.
You still got
work to do here.
You still have people who ain't met
the healed version
of you yet.

You still got songs to hum,
jokes to laugh at,
faces to light up just by showing up.

You don’t gotta see the morning
to know it’s coming.
You just gotta breathe till it does.

Stay.
Even if you're shaking.
Stay.
Even if you're tired.
Stay,
’cause somebody’s tomorrow is waiting on your today.

And when that sun climbs slow across your window,
let it find you still here-
soft, scarred,
but still shining.

’Cause the night be lying, baby.
But you-
You're the truth.

"Don't shape yourself
into the failed
visions of others.
You are the author of
your own story."
- Kaelin Smith

Therapeutic Letter Writing by Kaelin Smith
(Letter to Future Self)

I'm not who I was, but I'm not denying that I did what I did. I refused to let go, and she carried us here. The best is happening. It will come and you will accept it. I have so many things I want to achieve, and I will get there. You won't fall back into that rabbit hole that you were once in. If you do, you need to claw your way back up. I know you've grown since this was written. You will prosper. You will do great things for yourself, your loved ones, and, hopefully, your community. I trust that everything you will do will be for the good. I believe I can grow into who you are, what you will become, and whoever you plan to be. So, please do not give up on our goals, our plans, and don't ever stop wanting to be there for those who need you. Be the person I needed. Keep an open mind, always. Don't stop dreaming and setting goals. Carry our childhood selves. Don't lose your humor and playfulness. Carry your present self: someone who is working to do better for themselves. Whoever you are now, I know, is a good person. Never settle for less. Don't shape yourself into the failed visions of others. You are the author of your own story.

"Don't shape yourself into the failed visions of others.
You are the author of your own story."
- Kaelin Smith

Who Me
By Latoya Boyd

I heard somebody say, "Something is better than nothing, right?"
But after all I've been through, I was starting to think nothing is better than some...things, right?

I want to feel nothing because what I feel hurts too bad
Feeling like I want to die every time I cry,
because I must have gotten the Temu version of this game called life

Wrestling with thoughts of wanting to love myself
Wanting so desperately to reach out for help
Afraid of being judged for these feelings I felt

I sink deeper into my pain
I drown in this torrential rain
I draw blood from my own vein
I scream with no voice
I submit to having no choice
I visualize this low place as my peak
I lie down willingly on my bed of defeat

Weak...

Then I heard YOU speak...
You said, "I am the God that healeth thee!"
Who me?
You said, "I come that you might have life more abundantly?"
Who me?
You said, "Before you were formed in your mother's belly, I knew thee."
Who me?

You said, "We are troubled on every side, yet not distressed;
we are perplexed, but not in despair;
persecuted, but not forsaken;
cast down but not destroyed."
No, for real, me?
You said "I am He who was dead and behold, I am alive! Let me breathe life into you and show you why you should survive."

I said, "Go on, because I've lost the will and drive."
He said, "This is precisely why now is the time."

As He continued to speak, what I heard was life changing
I matter
My life matters
My pain is a matter for Him, not me
My pain has purpose that I can't yet see
My existence is divine and intentional
I can't take what's not mine.
He said, “I belong to Him, my soul is His...”
Then I realized, that's all I wanted the whole time.

IV. Addressing Suicide Risk Through Arts & Healing Education

Holding the Circle

Seven years ago, when I became a Certified Poetry Group Facilitator through Women Writing for (a) Change, I learned the quiet power of holding the circle or holding space. Over time, I've expanded those principles, shaping them into a framework that helps young people feel seen, supported, and ready to express themselves.

The first step is creating an inviting environment. If you're using single chairs, arranging them in a circle signals community, intention, and the absence of an unequal power dynamic. It removes the subtle hierarchy created when a facilitator sits at the head of a table and instead places everyone on equal ground. The next step is establishing safety. Everyone in the room, including the facilitator, should participate in the writing activity; this prevents observers and reinforces a sense of collective vulnerability. Remind the group that the space is confidential. The only exception is when someone expresses active suicide or homicide ideation that day. If so, that information must be shared to keep them or someone else safe. Past feelings, however, can be held and honored within the circle.

Working in diverse communities taught me how essential accessibility is. Many youths and teens avoid writing programs because literacy challenges, spoken or unspoken, make participation feel risky. Offer alternatives: drawing, creating "poetic pictures," or brainstorming silently with eyes closed until they're ready to contribute. Emphasize that hesitation isn't always about literacy; it may be shyness, difficulty expressing emotions, or discomfort writing in a group. If someone struggles to put words down, offer to be their scribe. When it's time to share, remind them that passing is allowed. They can share one line, just the topic they wrote about, or ask a trusted person to read for them. Because the true goal isn't perfect writing. It's building a circle where every person feels welcome to step forward in the way they can, in the moment they're ready. When a group learns to honor each voice on its own terms, something rare happens: the room becomes a place where healing, creativity, and trust can take root, and where young people discover that their stories are important and need to be heard.

Spirit Dancer **by Don Henry**

I Am My Own Healing
By Catrina Mills

I was born carrying stories
I never asked to hold—
memories braided into my blood,
whispers pressed into my bones.
They call it epigenetic trauma,
but I call it my grandmother's thunder,
my mother's uncried tears,
the weight of women who learned
to keep going when the world
kept taking.
I walk through this life
with ghosts that look like me—
ancestors humming warnings,
lessons, lullabies,
all at the same time.
Some days it feels like I'm fighting battles
that started before I ever had a name.
But still—
I rise inside it,
I breathe beyond it,
I break cycles with hands
that weren't supposed to be free.
I am the daughter of women
who taught themselves how to live
in spite of history.
Women who wiped their tears
with dignity,
stitched their hope into children,
and prayed courage into tomorrow.
Their pain did not end with them—
no—
it traveled, it followed,
it lived in me.

But so did their power.
So today, I choose myself.
I choose to stretch the ache
into understanding,
to turn survival into softness,
to let love be louder than the wounds I never earned.
I choose to breathe like my ribs
were never cages,
to trust my own becoming,
to forgive myself for carrying
what was never mine.
I am a Black woman
who remembers,
who resists,
who reclaims.
My story is not the trauma—
it is the transformation.
I am the first dream my ancestors get to see unfold.
I am the healing they prayed for
in the dark.
I am their victory walking,
speaking,
cooking,
loving,
living.
And no matter how heavy this world gets,
I am still here—
unbroken,
unburied,
unafraid.
Because I learned that survival
isn't just making it through—
it's learning how to live
like the sun chose you on purpose.
And baby,
it did.

Acceptance
By MoPoetry Phillips

I was told God bottles
every tear
Test show
my tear ducts
are blocked
Part of a condition called Sjogren's (Show Grins)
Ironic that I'd be forced to show grins
instead of tears
Fought to allow the emotions to surface
Pressed them down
for years
Hiding things
I'd been through
Kept captive my truth
Not allowing myself to say what's true
Didn't want to look like I had more scars than you
Quickly, I learned not to compare
Healing is just accepting your scars that are there
Ignorance is bliss
So, others aren't aware
Truth is, we all get stares.
But, it takes clarity to see things clearly
We are all preparing
on some level
Since healing is a continual journey
sometimes we look good on the outside,
but our soul's disheveled.
My tears may have stopped
flood warning
dam broken
bottles out of stock

Or maybe God is just showing me
He is through collecting
It's time for peace
Tears are relief
Release
This stage of grief
doesn't require tears.

CHE BUSIEK

"If you can provide clarity, you can bring back hope."

GROWTH

M I learn from my mistakes

I I can improve through hard work

N I never give up

D I am determined

S Success comes from self-reflection

E Effort will help me see improved results

T I always try my best

Surviving Mom Blog

Find You
By Jodie L. Summers

Find You:
HEAL it's going to take time...
It's not going to happen in your time, but it will in time.
HEAL no matter how long it takes, your journey is to Find You.
HEAL because you deserve it.
HEAL so they'll be 1 more person to show people the way.
HEAL so you can be happy without having to try.
HEAL it's going to take time...
No one can HEAL for you, so it's up to you to be the best version of yourself.
Stop ghosting yourself to give everyone else what you need and HEAL.
So, your trauma doesn't affect you in places you should be celebrating at HEAL.
Those tears of despair will only create puddles, until you HEAL and see the vast oceans of emotions that you've poured out into the world over your journey.
It's okay to feel lost, unwanted, misunderstood, wrong, ignorant and incomplete, but if you HEAL you will understand how all of that makes you unique and the main character of your story.
HEAL it's going to take time...
It's not going to be easy because the process of getting there was so traumatic it stopped you from loving on you properly, so HEAL and learn to love yourself better until it's no longer an action you have to take in desperation for your soul, but a part of you that you walk with every day.
HEAL it's not a process you have to take alone either, so stop closing off those that really mean you well. It's okay, because it's a part of the process of isolation and trauma from giving your trust to the wrong people and watching them misuse it, because they did not know the journey you were meant to take. But please, don't stay isolated forever, or you'll become hardened to all of those things that feed your inner child.
HEAL it's going to take time, but in life that is all we got and it's something precious enough to take a hold of.
HEAL so when love comes to find you it's not another battle that you have to fight trying to understand why someone needs you.

Conducting Therapeutic Letter Writing Sessions

By MoPoetry Phillips

Special Instructions: If you are writing a letter to someone other than yourself, we do not advise you to give the actual letter to the person. Therapeutic letter writing is intended for the writer only to help process through emotions, grief, hurt, and traumatic events, or to learn to uplift and encourage yourself.

Step # 1: Circle your selection(s) below

1. Letter to Myself: My Mind, My Body, My Spirit.
2. Letter to Someone Who is No Longer in Your Life (Deceased, Divorced, Breakup, Friendship Ended/Someone who Abandoned or Betrayed you)
3. Letter to Someone in My Family
4. Letter to My Past
5. Letter to My Future Self: My Mind, My Body, My Spirit, My Future Spouse/Family
6. Letter to My Dreams, Goals, Ambitions, and Purpose

<u>Writing Prompts for Each Section</u>

1. **Letter to Myself: My Mind, My Body, My Spirit:**
   - When writing this letter try to talk to yourself like you would your best friend or close loved one. Be kind to yourself. Sometimes it helps to write in 3rd person (referring to yourself by name and using she/her/they or whatever pronouns you use). For example: Dear MoPoetry: You are worthy. You are loved.
   - Give thanks for your mind, your strength, your focus, determination, your ability to make decisions, your skills and strengths…
   - Encourage your body. You are beautiful… You are perfect as you are… You are getting better every day…
2. **Letter to Someone Who is No Longer in Your Life (Deceased, Divorced, Breakup, Friendship Ended/Someone who Abandoned or Betrayed you)**
   - Dear____; I'm writing you this letter, because it really hurt me when you…
   - It hurts that you are gone….
   - You betrayed/abandoned me…
   - You weren't worth me, my time, or my energy…
   - I thought it would last forever….

Conducting Therapeutic Letter Writing Sessions (cont.)
#2 cont.

- You betrayed me and it made me feel….
- I forgive you, but I will never trust you again, because….
- Having you walk out my life caused me to….
- I wish you knew and understood how it made me feel….

3. **Letter to Someone in My Family(brother/sister/mother/father/cousin)**
    - We are family, but I feel like…
    - I'm sorry that….
    - I regret that….
    - It's not my fault that…
    - I forgive you for…..
    - I accept that….

4. **Letter to My Past**
    - My past is my past…
    - You cannot hold me hostage by my past…
    - I forgive myself for my past decisions….
    - My past does not define me, because….
    - My past was part of my process, because…
    - I see my past as….

5. **Letter to My Future Self: My Mind, My Body, My Spirit, My Future Spouse/Family**
    - The best is yet to come….
    - My latter, or the rest of my life will be better than what I've experienced…
    - I have great things coming in my future….
    - Everything I've dreamed is coming to pass….
    - I will prosper…
    - My body/health will align with the vision I have for the rest of my life…

Conducting Therapeutic Letter Writing Sessions (cont.)

6. **Letter to My Dreams, Goals, Ambitions, and Purpose**
    - All the good seeds I've planted will blossom in its perfect timing…
    - I am capable and I will accomplish all my goals…
    - My work is not in vain….
    - I am walking the divine purpose for my life…
    - I am on track, focused, and headed in the right direction…
    - Doors open for me…
    - Opportunities come to me…
    - Unmerited/undeserved things happen to me, and I welcome it to happen.
    - I'm not afraid of greatness…
    - I have everything I need….

Anticipation of the Hunt **by Don Henry**

Poetry Tools
line breaks
writing in shorter lines to slow the reader down
rhythm
makes you tap your foot
simile
comparing using 'like' or "as"
metaphor
saying that one thing is something else
personification
giving human traits to something that is not human
imagery
helping the reader form a picture in their mind
alliteration
using the same sound at the beginning of neighboring words
repetition
repeating something
THE CLASSROOM KEY

Using Poetry Tools for Arts & Healing Work (cont.)

1. **Line Breaks**- Telling your truth in written form is hard work. Writing every detail chronologically can be triggering and emotionally taxing. Short line breaks are not only an indicator that differentiates written stories or prose from poetry, but they are also what makes poetry unique and easily distinguishable when seen on the page. When helping clients write through their pain offer them the freedom to use sentence fragments, or fewer words. Invite them to write in a stream of consciousness that welcomes and invites their hearts and minds to record whatever comes without judgement. Tell them that everything does not have to make sense, rhyme, or sound poetic. The point is to bring what they need to the surface, so that they can become aware of anything that needs healing. Sometimes it is just one sentence on an entire page of writing that will give clues about what is needed.
2. **Metaphor**- A common Alaskan metaphor is that the bear means strength. Metaphors are a type of symbolism that directly compares two normally unrelated things unlike a simile which compares them using "like" or "as." Imagine telling your student to compare bullying to drowning instead of just writing about what it feels like being bullied. First, have them write down all the water reference words they can think of: **trickled, poured, flooded**, and **capsize**. Then, have them use those words to attach to the events or feelings they experience. They may say:

    The mean words **trickled** in at first,
    tiny drops I try to ignore.
    Then they **poured** over me
    when the teasing starts again.
    Sometimes it **flooded**,
    too big for me to push away.
    And on the hardest days,
    it might **capsize**,
    tilting under all that hurt.
    But when someone is kind,
    a strong hand in the water lifts me back up
    helps me float again.

Using Poetry Tools for Arts & Healing Work (cont.)

3. **Imagery**- When recalling good experiences or even writing about the future, encouraging your writing group to use imagery will not only strengthen their writing, but it will also strengthen the vision. This makes storytelling more immersive by helping them use their sense of smell, sight, sound, touch, and taste.
4. **Repetition**- To use repetition in writing, you can have the student pick one important line that they will repeat. This line can be inserted in various places within the writing. The most common is the first line of each stanza, or paragraph, caused by intentional line breaks. Repetition reinforces what you hear, helps make declarations, gives voice and helps rehearse affirmations.
5. **Rhythm-** This is the internal beat or flow within the writing. Creating rhythm can become a technical process for professional writers, but within the writing circle it can be used loosely and celebrated by allowing space for each writer to read or speak their thoughts. It is a chance for them to hear the rhythm created by their voice. Reading a loud helps you hear rhythm more clearly than just silently reading it to yourself.
6. **Simile**- Is similar to a metaphor, because it compares two abstracts (unlike things), but it uses the words "like" or "as." Using the same poem in #2 above, I rewrote this one using similes. This is especially useful when doing trauma work, because it gives comparison to things not easily explained.

> The mean words **trickled** in at first,
> like tiny drops I try to ignore.
> Then they **poured** over me
> when the teasing starts again.
> Sometimes it feels like a **flood**,
> too big for me to push away.
> And on the hardest days,
> I feel like I might **capsize**, tilting under all that hurt.
> But when someone is kind,
> it's like a strong hand in the water,
> lifting me back up, helping me float again

Using Poetry Tools for Arts & Healing Work (cont.)

7. **Personification-** A literary device that gives non-human things human characteristics. It reminds me of the saying, "If these walls could talk." Think about your best family memory. If the walls could retell the story, what would they say?
8. **Alliteration-** Alliteration is having the same letter or sounds at the beginning of closely connected words on the page. It is easy to explain when it accidentally occurs when writing. Later, after pointing it out, the writer can begin to ease their way into intentionally using it as a technique.

Close Readings

Short-form content and rapid scrolling have reduced our collective attention span. Many people struggle to retell what they've just heard or seen. Close readings strengthen comprehension by slowing the pace and helping participants truly listen. Use the poems given within the book as text for your close readings.

- **To facilitate a close reading:**
  - Invite someone in the circle to read the poem aloud.
  - Before they begin, let the group know you will read the poem a second time for a close reading focused on themes, tone, and key lines.
  - This reassurance helps the first reader relax, knowing the responsibility for interpretation isn't on them alone.
- **During the close reading:**
  - Go line by line through the poem.
  - If it uses rhyme, consider reading rhyming lines or couplets together.
  - Restate lines in clear, accessible language to support understanding.
  - Highlight strong word choices or moments of emotional weight.
  - Move slowly and intentionally so the group can absorb the writer's meaning and message.

Thematic Focus

Technique # 1 - Before doing a reading or listening to a poem from this book, ask youth or teens to listen for themes, or what the poem is about. Then after reading, say the themes together or list them on the board.

Technique # 2 – This strategy takes some preplanning. Read the poem yourself at home. Take 4-5 lines from the poem and write them on individual strips of paper. Choose lines that are very strong and would create good dialogue. Make sure to number each strip as they appear in the poem. Put those strips into a quart or gallon size storage bag. When you are in class or group, read the poem out loud. Then, ask for 4-5 volunteers to volunteer to take a line from the poem out of the bag, and call upon #1 to read the line they selected. Ask them to give you feedback on that line by telling them to say whatever that line means to them. After they answer, give the entire class a chance to give input as well. Next, call on the person who selected #2, and so on. This increases engagement and aids with comprehension.

Guide to Leading Visual Art Analysis Workshops
By MoPoetry Phillips

1. After you select the picture, painting, or visual art image, look at it carefully in a well-lit, quiet place and prepare to take notes of what you see for each section below. Don Henry's original artwork which is included in this publication is the perfect material needed to conduct a visual art analysis.

2. What does the title of the visual art piece say about what the creator is trying to tell you through their work?

3. Pay attention to the main subject, objects, and /or person in the visual art piece. Think about what the person is wearing. Does it give you clues to what year, age it depicts? Record what you find.

4. What is the purpose of objects, animals, etc.? How does it help tell the story?

5. Look at color, shadows, and lighting. Does it create a certain mood or tone, make you feel happy or sad?

6. NOW with all that, the most important thing is what you are feeling. How do you connect with the piece? Is there something in your life or that you have experienced that helps you connect with the piece? Does the piece speak to world issues, issues within your culture, or social justice, especially issues that we are still fighting to overcome?

7. Breathe, believe in yourself, and trust your instinct.

8. Make sure the words you choose are things that anyone else can easily understand. Allow others to read it and give you advice to know if it makes sense to them.

9. After you take time to do your analysis and record information, try to use the information to write a poem based on the visual arts piece.

V. Support for Those Who Do the Work

The Why That Holds You: Protecting Yourself in the Work

It is essential to understand why you are dedicating your time, energy, and skills to any profession or career path. Knowing your "why" gives purpose to your actions, guides your decisions, and sustains your motivation, even during challenging moments. This is particularly critical when working with youth, especially those experiencing crisis or trauma. In these settings, the emotional demands, unpredictability, and intensity of the work can be overwhelming, and without a clear understanding of your underlying purpose, it is easy to become discouraged or burned out. Keeping your "why" at the forefront allows you to stay grounded, maintain empathy, and consistently approach each interaction with focus, patience, and intentionality. It also serves as a compass, reminding you that your efforts, no matter how small they may seem, can have a profound impact on the lives of the young people you serve.

Stay
By Michael "Double G" Kielanowicz

You…
The one reading these lines
The one that feels like they're losing their grip
on all that matters
I need you to know that your matter matters
I don't mean to be intrusive
But this isn't the time for me to mind my manners
So
I'm going to speak like I've been spoken through
This is a message to the chosen few
You were born for better
Birthed for more than this Earth has allowed you to be
Search yourself for the you that lies beyond all that you see
Until your self-image becomes clearer
You were made to reflect light like a mirror
How dare the world doubt you
They fear what they don't understand
By design you're as intricate in detail as a single grain of sand
I dare you conform your will in accordance with God's plan
We are in this world not of it
It's ok to live this life and not love it
Put you first
Place nobody else above it
When the pushback comes
Shove it
Remain defiant
What's a silent treatment to a sleeping giant
Every day
I dare you to
Arise a rose that serves a God that arose with all power in His Hand
Stand for the life you deserve
Stranger in a foreign land
Where your footsteps aren't welcomed
Stand on His Word
What God has Spoken about your life will not return to Him void
The blood still works
Remain gainfully employed

Stay on your job
Emulate Job
Until you every utterance is profession
Watch your curses turn to blessings
The body needs you
What's a head without the feet
My soul can't bear to see you suffer the agony of defeat
Please stay
Trouble comes like a thief in the night
Often without warning
But like clockwork
Remember
Before there were ashes
There were embers
Joy comes in the morning
Reignite that fire that reminded you to be
A phoenix so rooted in faith you take flight
because you're spiritually grounded like the trees
The journey from Boys II Men starts on bended knee
Chase your purpose
On purpose
Never stray
Be the change you wish to see
Help me welcome the new day

How Do You See Yourself Successfully Helping Others Combat Suicide?

Clarity
Competence
Constraints
Concentration
Creativity
Courage
Continuous Learning

It may seem weird to talk about success and suicide prevention work in the same sentence. However, whether we feel effective or successful in this line of work can cause a lot of stress. Over the years, there are several people who have defined what success looks like. These 7 terms: clarity, competence, constraints, concentration, creativity, courage, and continuous learning are taken from Brian Tracy's "Seven Seas of Success." Feel free to Google and find a more detailed explanation of each definition if you need help. Take 15 minutes and think about one or more of these terms that stand out for you. Write how you see yourself helping others combat suicide. Think about how that falls under 1-2 areas of success? I wanted to start with success, but let's be honest, what would make you feel like a failure in this line of work? This would be a good time to think about whether the department where you work celebrates your wins, or positive progress. If not, is there anything you can suggest putting into practice from this point forward to help celebrate your wins?

Self-Care: How to Prevent Binge Working?

Full-time, forty-hour weeks have been a societal norm since Ford Motor Company adopted it in the 1920's with the goal of working 8-hour days. However, mental health workers, Peer Recovery Supporters, Behavioral Health Specialists, nurses, and educators who spend countless hours outside of class time working on lesson planning tend to work more than 8 hours a day. Also, what tends to happen with those working in the fields listed above is binge working. Some days you are working 12, 14, or 16 hours a day causing you to collapse into days of inactivity in between due to being overwhelmed.

As we start the discussion of self-care, think about the total time each day you spend working. Do you have a cut-off time when you are off the clock, or are you always on call? Also, since self-care is about your entire self, think about the rest of your life commitments. Do you have a large family that requires you to spend time cooking and washing clothes all the time? Do you have younger children that require extra clean-up time around the house? Do you have support? Do you have problems setting boundaries, telling people when you are overextended, or that you don't have the capacity to take on anything else?

Copy the handout "Take Care of Yourself" on page 120. Take at least 20 minutes to complete it. Make sure to include things that honor your culture, interests, local environment, and traditions. For example, spending time on the land, subsistence activities, storytelling, and spiritual practices. Take this seriously, because this self-care plan will be your first line of defense for avoiding burnout, or emotional, mental, physical exhaustion that can be caused while doing suicide prevention work. I call it "work", to keep us grounded in the idea that despite our passion and strong desire to help, it is work indeed.

FOR YOUR MIND

FOR YOUR BODY

FOR YOUR SPIRITUAL

Index (Poems by Authors & Page Numbers)

Index (Page Numbers for Visual Art Pieces by Don Henry)

Index (Reasons Youth and Teens Attempt and/or Die by Suicide)

Poverty, Injustice, & Social-economic Stressors

- Poverty, homelessness, unavailable or inadequate housing, and job loss
- Injustice and discrimination
- Social-economic struggle, lack of health resources, and lack of educational opportunities
- Overwhelming real-life pressures with limited support from family and community support
- Isolation
- Lack of healthy resources

Feeling Unheard or Invalidated

- Their voices and feelings aren't heard, especially within their families and communities (This is really true if their viewpoints are different.)
- Adults dismiss or invalidate their feelings.
- Even when adults offer help, youth have a hard time accepting help due to lack of trust
- Not being listened to or taken seriously
- They need us to do more than see them. They want us to hear them.
- They feel invisible
- Youth and teens don't know how to express themselves, so they engage in negative coping skills and risky behaviors.

Lack of Coping Skills & Emotional Regulation

- Not learning or applying coping techniques
- Not knowing how to handle loss, failure, rejection, and disappointment
- Not knowing how to have self-compassion
- Not knowing how to cope with childhood trauma
- Living in a "crash out" world where everything feels like a crisis (catastrophizing)
- Negative generalizations about life
- Not forming healthy relationships

Reasons Youth and Teens Attempt and/or Die by Suicide (cont.)

Loneliness, Isolation, & Not Finding Their Tribe

- Not having anyone who understands, listens, or relates
- Loneliness, depression, and low mood
- Not finding their tribe leading to a sense of isolation
- Having no place to safely be themselves or express themselves
- Low self-esteem
- Lack of resources or groups for connection to support

Trauma Exposure (Personal, Family, or Community)

- Childhood trauma
- Witnessing suicide of others
- Generational trauma
- Experiences of abuse, neglect, or bullying
- Punished when speaking native language & encouraged to stop
- Sexual abuse
- Elder abuse
- Alcohol and drug use
- Past silent treatment
- Past historical traumatic experience.
    - For example, past teachers, Bureau of Indian Affairs (BIA's) treatment toward students, or missionaries forced Alaskan Natives/American Indians to attend churches.
- Cultural differences (native people v. more westernized views)
- Problems finding balance with progression from more traditional ways to new cultural norms
- Parental influence
- Not being open towards others
- Grief/deaths
- Suicide taboo in the Alaskan Native/American Indian culture
- Confusion over spiritual beliefs
- Afraid to be themselves
- Mental, emotional, physical, spiritual isolation
- An internal mistrust of their own abilities or instincts
- Feeling lost within their own culture even despite meeting certain life goals.

Reasons Youth and Teens Attempt and/or Die by Suicide (cont.)

Mental Health Stigmas & Cultural Barriers

- Mental health stigma in families, communities, and villages, especially Alaskan Native, American Indian, and African American communities.
- Being raised to believe that "What goes on in this house, stays in this house."
- Dismissing depression, and anxiety as attitude or drama.
- Families rejecting therapy, because "Jesus will fix it."
- Belief that faith alone should solve mental health struggles
- Cultural influences (past and present) contributing to family separation
- Feeling like they are living in two words (western/modern) and traditional
- Guilt from their current views conflicting with traditional values
- Struggling with integration and the pressure to fit in
- Current silent treatment
- Judgement from peers
- Overthinking about their own lives
- Everyone knows everyone
- Fear of judgment
- Belief that mental health issues are a sign of weakness
- Isolation
- Feeling unaccepted
- Being seen only from one viewpoint
- Not being able to express their full self

Social Media Pressure & Unrealistic Standards

- Lack of self-worth, feeling they're not enough due to social media
- Constant comparison and perceived inadequacy
- Feeling attacked or defensive due to people only seeing one side
- Being ganged up on for their beliefs
- Cyberbullying
- Seeing unexpected news of death or tragedy

Reasons Youth and Teens Attempt and/or Die by Suicide (cont.)

Hopelessness & Lack of Future Vision

- Not seeing a future
- Feeling like there's no path forward
- Some youth being very aware of themselves and deciding they don't want to be in the world
- Lack of opportunities: work, education, & career path/development
- Lack of support for connection

Lack of Supportive Relationships & Safe Adults

- No mentors or trusted adults
- Adults missing signs of distress, turning a blind eye
- Feeling youth or teens are "too young to feel that" or don't know what they are talking about
- Not having anywhere safe to express themselves
- Wanting connection, but not receiving it
- Feeling trapped due to being in a rural area. For example, if teens or youth don't feel supported in rural areas, they are more likely to feel trapped and unsafe.

About the Visual Artist

Don Henry is an Alaska-based visual artist whose work traces the quiet pulse of the North: its light, landforms, and the human stories woven through them. Drawing from decades of life in Alaska's rural and urban communities, Henry creates paintings and mixed-media pieces that honor both cultural memory and the changing environment. His practice often blends traditional techniques with contemporary forms, creating textured narratives that echo the state's rugged beauty and its resilient people.

Henry's art has been featured in regional exhibitions, community projects, and educational spaces that center Alaska Native experience, land stewardship, and youth empowerment. Whether capturing the subtle shift of seasonal light or the lived realities of Alaska's diverse communities, Henry's work invites viewers into a space of reflection and belonging. He continues to create from his home in Alaska, committed to amplifying local voices and preserving the stories that shape the North.

About the Author

MoPoetry Phillips is a Cincinnati-based writer, educator, and arts advocate whose work weaves creative expression with community healing. As founder of Arts Equity Collective, she develops arts-based programs that uplift marginalized voices, expand access to creative opportunities, and support prevention education on suicide, domestic violence, and gun violence. Her workshops and curricula are used by behavioral health specialists, educators, and youth and adult serving organizations nationwide.

She has been published by the Cincinnati Review, Ghosn Publishing, Word Press, Poets Against Racism and Hate, the Voices Project, and self-published her books Equals Greatness and Arts Equity Collective presents: SOS Empowerment Arts & Healing (A Book of Poetry & Visual Art About Survivors' Stories). She has been highlighted in the Cincinnati Enquirer, Cincinnati Herald, and Street Vibes newspapers; Urban One and WAIFM Radio; WCVG, WCPO, WXIX, WLWT and WVXU news.

A poet with a resonant stage presence, Phillips transforms lived experience into work that fosters dialogue, empathy, and restoration. Her leadership emphasizes youth empowerment and trauma-informed practice, ensuring young people, especially those navigating foster care, cultural displacement, or systemic inequities are heard, held, and creatively supported. For booking information, please email: mopoetry@artsequitycollective.org.

www.ingramcontent.com/pod-product-compliance
Lightning Source LLC
LaVergne TN
LVHW060640110826
845147LV00018B/1014

* 9 7 9 8 9 9 9 1 7 8 3 2 9 *